THE DAM BUSTERS

BREAKING THE GREAT DAMS OF WESTERN GERMANY 16–17 MAY 1943

DEDICATION

To my dear father
DAVID DUNBAR FALCONER
Father, friend, fellow author and inspiration

19 April 1934 – 8 January 2002

THE DAM BUSTERS

BREAKING THE GREAT DAMS OF WESTERN GERMANY 16–17 MAY 1943

JONATHAN FALCONER

FOREWORD BY
RICHARD TODD

SUTTON PUBLISHING

First published in the United Kingdom in 2003 by
Sutton Publishing Limited · Phoenix Mill
Thrupp · Stroud · Gloucestershire · GL5 2BU

This paperback edition first published in 2005

British Library Cataloguing in Publication Data
A catalogue record for this book is available from the British
Library.

ISBN 0-7509-4003-4

Typeset in 12/15 Sabon MT.
Typesetting and origination by
Sutton Publishing Limited.
Printed and bound in England by
J.H. Haynes & Co. Ltd, Sparkford.

CONTENTS

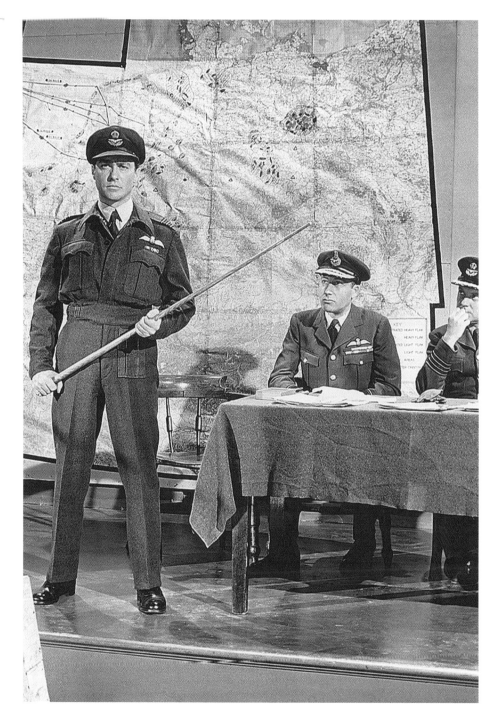

Richard Todd as W/C Guy Gibson in the film *The Dam Busters.*

(Canal+Image)

FOREWORD

by

RICHARD TODD OBE

I had the honour and good fortune to be cast as Guy Gibson in the epic film *The Dam Busters*. Preparations and research for the project had lasted two years before filming started in 1954, and during that period I readied myself to play Gibson by discussions with his widow, his father, various acquaintances and former members of 617 Squadron, besides reading all the material I could get hold of, including of course his own book, *Enemy Coast Ahead*, and Paul Brickhill's *The Dam Busters*, on which the film is based.

I wish now that Jonathan Falconer's book had been available to me. It would have added greatly to my knowledge and understanding of the events of the night of 16–17 May 1943, and the preparations for and aftermath of that historic attack on the great dams of western Germany.

A wealth of detail and meticulous research has been encapsulated into Mr Falconer's book in such a very readable style that I have read and re-read the work with enthusiasm and real pleasure.

I am sure that this latest description of the dam busters will be riveting for all those who take a keen interest in Second World War history, in the achievements of RAF Bomber Command and in the British film industry.

ACKNOWLEDGEMENTS

Four books have been invaluable to me in researching and writing this short account of 617 Squadron's dams raids. Of these, the two most important were Guy Gibson's own account of the build-up to Operation Chastise and the attack itself, in *Enemy Coast Ahead*, first published in 1946, and John Sweetman's *The Dambusters Raid*, first published in 1982.

Enemy Coast Ahead covers the whole of Gibson's RAF operational flying career with 50, 29, 106 and then 617 Squadrons. His account of the dams raid itself is, therefore, a fairly short appreciation, occupying only three chapters out of eighteen, albeit from the unique perspective of the leader of the raid and one who was actually *there*. However, there is now some speculation as to whether some of Gibson's writing was guided by the hidden hands of ghost writers at the Ministry of Information and Air Ministry. Even if this is the case, *Enemy Coast Ahead* still makes compelling reading because it is the story of one of Britain's top bomber pilots of the Second World War, and positively reeks of the atmosphere of the period.

John Sweetman's *The Dambusters Raid* is a scholarly and highly detailed account of the background to Chastise, the attack and its aftermath. This book is probably as good as it gets about the dams raid, in terms of both depth of research and level of detail incorporated into the narrative. Not only has Sweetman consulted a wealth of primary sources of information during the course of his research, but he has also interviewed many of the survivors of the dams raid – back-room boffins and 617 Squadron ground crew, as well as Barnes Wallis and aircrew survivors themselves.

Paul Brickhill's classic, *The Dam Busters* (1951), and Helmuth Euler's *The Dams Raid Through the Lens* (2001) were also of considerable help to me. Brickhill researched *The Dam Busters* soon after the end of the war, when many of the main characters were still alive and the momentous events they had helped to shape were still fresh in their minds. Euler's work is very much the dams raid as seen from the German perspective. First published in German in 1992 as *Wasserkrieg*, it is the story of the raid through the lenses of the photographers who recorded the Chastise story before, during and after the operation, supporting many fascinating German eyewitness accounts.

It is a great privilege to have the foreword for this book written by the distinguished film and stage actor Richard Todd, who played Guy Gibson in Michael Anderson's stirring account of Operation Chastise, *The Dam Busters*.

The photographic archive of the former Road and Transport Research Laboratory is a truly massive and engrossing pictorial resource that only now is beginning to see the light of day. Hopefully, once this material has been assessed and catalogued, it will be available to a wider audience beyond the civil servants and road engineers for whom it was intended. I am very grateful to Richard Ibbitt, chief photographer of TRL Ltd (formerly the Road and Transport Research Laboratory), for allowing me access to some of this incredible collection, and for his interest in this book.

Margaret Jones and Kinnie Desai of the National Physical Laboratory at Teddington are also to be thanked for tracking down a photograph of No. 2 Ship Tank in which Barnes Wallis carried out trials on golf-ball-size models of the bouncing bomb. The photograph is reproduced by kind permission of the Controller of Crown Copyright.

Paul Couper is the talented technical illustrator responsible for the fabulous three-view scale drawings of the Avro Lancaster B Mk I (Type 464 Provisioning). Paul is available for commissions and can be contacted at 58 Kimbolton Road, Portsmouth, Hants PO3 6BZ.

Thanks are also due to fellow authors and enthusiasts: Dr Alfred Price, Bruce Robertson and Richard Simms for searching their own photograph collections and for allowing me to reproduce illustrations obtained from these sources; Graham Pitchfork for assistance with gallantry awards information; Ian Thirsk at the RAF Museum for his ready assistance with some points of detail concerning the film *The Dam Busters*; photographer and author Richard Winslade for permission to reproduce the superb photograph of the BBMF Lancaster; and the acclaimed aviation artist Nicolas Trudgian and the Military Gallery, Bath, for kind permission to reproduce Nick's two wonderfully evocative paintings.

I am grateful to Paul Baillie, military researcher, who procured copies for me of the award citations for Guy Gibson and Ken Brown from the Public Record Office.

My friend and work colleague Bow Watkinson has been a great source of advice and guidance when it came to picture selection. Thanks are due to him and to fellow colleague Martin Latham for creating the diagrams and maps that appear in this book.

John Herron of Canal+Image UK was enthusiastic and helpful in tracking down stills photographs from the film *The Dam Busters*, and for providing copies of the original film poster and souvenir book from his company's archives. They are reproduced here by kind permission of Canal+Image UK.

The Bundesarchiv, Germany, the Imperial War Museum, London, the RAF Museum, Hendon, Atlantic Syndication and the Royal Society (Godfrey Argent) have also been very helpful in providing many of the photographs that illustrate the pages that follow: the photographs from their respective collections are reproduced with their kind permission. In the case of the museums, individual copies can be obtained by contacting the relevant institutions at the addresses below and quoting the full negative reference number.

Bundesarchiv
Potsdamer Strasse 1, 56075 Koblenz, Germany

www.bundesarchiv.de

Imperial War Museum
Department of Photographs, Lambeth Road, London SE1 6HZ

www.iwm.org.uk

RAF Museum
Photographic Department, Hendon, London NW9 2LL

www.rafmuseum.org.uk

INTRODUCTION

Thanks to a 1955 film called *The Dam Busters* that thrilled cinema audiences the length and breadth of Britain, a wartime exploit of an elite RAF bomber squadron assumed legendary status almost overnight. It is doubtful whether any other RAF squadron – or indeed any flying unit in any other air force – could have achieved such fame for a single operation, then or now. The squadron in question is, of course, No. 617, and the operation was the attack in May 1943 by nineteen Avro Lancasters on the Möhne, Eder and Sorpe dams in western Germany, using Barnes Wallis's revolutionary bouncing bomb.

In the eyes of the wartime British press, and later of author Paul Brickhill and the Associated British Picture Corporation, 617 Squadron and Operation 'Chastise' (as the attack on the Ruhr dams was code-named) certainly had all the ingredients of a classic war story – a miracle weapon, an eccentric inventor, a secret squadron formed from the very best crews the RAF could muster, and a seemingly impossible task of destroying a clutch of hitherto unassailable targets. Success in the task would almost certainly alter the course of the war; but the end result was a pyrrhic victory. Two of the three main targets were destroyed, a Victoria Cross was awarded to the squadron's gallant leader, and an unsustainable casualty rate saw nearly half of 617's crews killed. The horrendous aircrew losses bore out Bomber Harris's warning that low-level attacks using heavy bombers were recipes for disaster; but the raids moved the irascible bomber baron to grudgingly acknowledge the justification of Bomber Command's existence that they so clearly upheld.

Born sixteen years after the war's end, I have no direct personal experience of the famous dams raid, but, like many boys of my generation, a passion for the exploits of Guy Gibson and his dam busters was stirred through eagerly reading Paul Brickhill's classic account of 617 Squadron at war. In what I believe was its first airing on television, the BBC screened Michael Anderson's peerless film, *The Dam Busters*, over the Whitsun bank holiday in May 1971. At a little before eight in the evening on Sunday 29 May, my father switched on our black and white television set and the family settled down to watch Richard Todd and Michael Redgrave re-enact this epic story. For two hours the film held me spellbound, and its effect on me thereafter was deep and far-reaching.

Soon afterwards I rushed out to my local model shop in Bath, the Modeller's Den, to buy the Revell 1/72nd-scale plastic model kit of Guy Gibson's Lancaster, G for George. Several years later, when I had a little more pocket money to spare, the giant 1/48th-scale dam buster Lancaster was purchased and, after weeks of careful gluing and painting, it took pride of place in my bedroom. What it was to gaze intently at these inanimate plastic leviathans on my chest of drawers and imagine myself up in the cockpit of G for George, alongside Guy Gibson, with the deafening sound of four Merlins reverberating in my ears, red-hot flak zipping past the cockpit, assisting him with the throttles on the run-in across the Möhne lake.

Over Sunday tea, I recall hearing my grandfather talk about the dams raid and of some of the men involved whom he had known or met during his thirty-four years in the RAF. As an engineering officer during the Second World War he had been closely involved at RAE Farnborough, and then at RAF Benson, with the development of the Spitfire and Mosquito for photo-reconnaissance use. In the course of this work I believe he had met Guy Gibson, albeit very briefly, as well as the PR pilots whom he had known well and who had flown from Benson on the pre- and post-dams raid reconnaissance flights. During the early 1950s my grandfather had also known dam buster Ivan Whittaker when they were both serving with the RAF in the Suez Canal Zone. Whittaker had been Mick Martin's flight engineer on the dams raid.

As a young boy, links with these Titans who had moulded aviation history were such stuff as dreams were made of. However tenuous, these associations served to deepen my interest in Operation Chastise, and in RAF history generally. The opportunity to write this book is thus a childhood dream come true.

At this point, however, I should point out that it is intended neither as the definitive account of the raid, nor seeks to offer new or controversial interpretations. Rather, I hope that the book will be received as an accessible narrative account of the dam buster legend, supported by a strong and well-presented selection of photographs and illustrations. But an added problem to the telling of such a well-known story is the dearth of action photographs depicting the raid itself. Owing to the extreme secrecy surrounding Chastise, only nine official photographs were taken – and these were on the ground at Scampton – before and after the raid, of which only four were passed for publication by the censor. What happened to the remaining five is anyone's guess, although I suspect they were destroyed. Thus, what was probably the RAF's most famous operation of the Second World War became the least photographed. Perhaps this adds to the power of the dam busters legend.

Jonathan Falconer
Bradford-on-Avon
September 2002

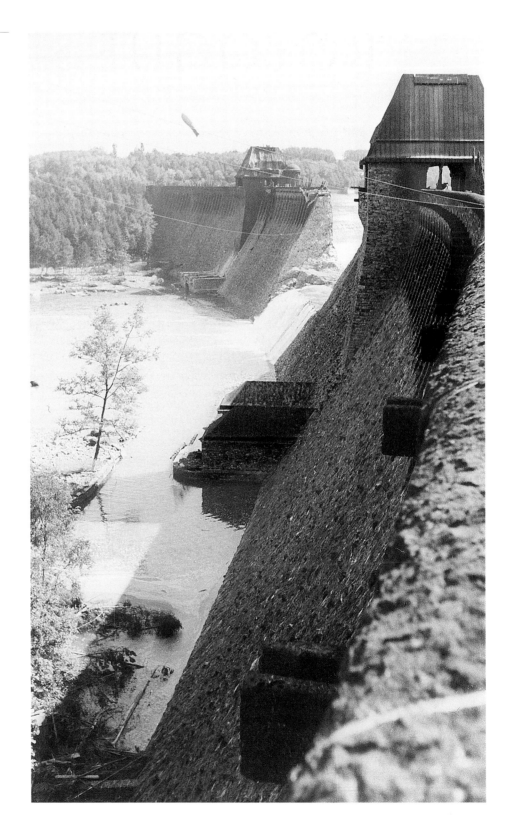

Devastation at the Möhne dam.
(Bundesarchiv 1011/637/4192/27)

PROLOGUE

One hour to go, and one hour left before Germany, one hour of peace before flak. I thought to myself: here are 133 boys who have got an hour to live before going through hell. Some of them won't get back. It won't be me – you never think you are not coming back. We won't all get back, but who is it will be unlucky out of these 133 men?

Guy Gibson in *Enemy Coast Ahead,* 1946

In the early hours of this morning a force of Lancasters attacked with mines the dams at the Möhne and Sorpe reservoirs. . . The Eder dam was also attacked and reported as breached. . . The attacks were pressed home from a very low level with great determination and coolness in the face of fierce resistance.

Air Ministry communiqué, 17 May 1943

Bomber Command have struck deep, and their achievement may well alarm the Reich. Successful air attack on a large dam was considered not long ago impossible. Germany will learn that other things outside the calculations of the Luftwaffe are now possible to the Allied Air Forces.

Leading article in the *Daily Telegraph,* 18 May 1943

I was overcome by the immensity of it [the inundation] and when I realised what had happened I just wondered if the powers that be realised just how much damage had been done.

F/O Jerry Fray, RAF photo-reconnaissance pilot, 17 May 1943

The British came close to a success which would have been greater than anything they had achieved hitherto with a commitment of thousands of bombers.

Albert Speer, Hitler's Armaments Minister

CHAPTER 1

STRIKING BACK

THE RAF'S EARLY BOMBING OFFENSIVE

Two days after Hitler's forces invaded Poland in September 1939, Britain declared war on Nazi Germany. At home, as the blackout went up and sandbags were piled high, Britons steeled themselves for the war that now lay ahead. While civilians learnt to live with rationing and shortages, the RAF was faced with the problem of how to wage an effective strategic air offensive against Germany with so few and inadequate aircraft: on any given day, only 280 were serviceable and with crews. Air Chief Marshal Sir Edgar Ludlow-Hewitt, then Commander-in-Chief of Bomber Command,

Below: A scene of well-ordered activity surrounds this 110 Squadron Bristol Blenheim light bomber at Wattisham in Norfolk as it is refuelled and bombed up for another sortie in the invasion summer of 1940. Blenheims and their crews suffered an alarmingly high casualty rate during the daylight raids against enemy targets in the first years of war. (IWM CH364)

1

tried in vain to open the eyes of the Air Staff to the serious shortcomings in aircraft, armament and equipment, and not least aircrew training at even the most basic level. After the first costly daylight bombing raids on enemy targets in September and December 1939, the pre-war theory that the bomber would always get through was quickly proved wrong, and Bomber Command realised that if it wanted to avoid heavy casualties, the only way to pursue an effective bombing campaign was under cover of darkness.

During the winter of 1940/1 it was believed that bombing raids on the small but vital enemy oil refineries in the Ruhr Valley would reduce Germany to impotence. While the attacks proved a dismal failure, the first signs of the future 'area offensive' were in evidence on 16 December 1940, when the centre and suburbs of the city of Mannheim were bombed. By March 1941, however, the U-boat menace in the Atlantic Ocean had reached crisis point and Bomber Command was diverted for three months from direct attacks on Germany to bomb

Above: These Wellington crews of 149 Squadron have just returned to their base at Mildenhall following the RAF's raid on Berlin of 25 August 1940.

(IWM HU44271)

3

enemy naval targets elsewhere, in the hope of relieving the wolf packs' stranglehold on the Atlantic convoy supply routes to Britain.

With its aircrew untrained and untried in night bombing, it was not until mid-1941 that Bomber Command was forced to face up to its grave shortcomings. The Butt Report of August 1941, commissioned by Prime Minister Winston Churchill's scientific adviser, Lord Cherwell, revealed that few if any of its bombers had reached what they thought was the target, and fewer still had actually dropped their bombs anywhere near it. Hundreds of brave aircrew had died in the process, and to little effect. But with the formation in 1942 of a specialist target -

finding and marking force, 8 (Pathfinder) Group, the first of several measures was taken to remedy this situation. The Pathfinders' task was to guide squadrons of the main bomber force to the target, which they had marked in advance with coloured flares and target indicators, thereby enabling accurate bombing to take place.

However, the problems encountered by the Command's heavy bomber squadrons of finding and hitting a target by night did not stop the medium bomber squadrons of 2 Group from continuing to mount daring but often costly daylight raids against enemy targets in occupied Europe and in Germany itself: locating a target in daylight and hitting it with bombs from low level did not pose the same problems for navigation and bombing accuracy as a night-bombing operation over a longer distance and at high altitude. From May 1943, control of 2 Group passed from Bomber Command to the 2nd Tactical Air Force, in preparation for the Allied invasion of north-west Europe, and from thereon the Command became an exclusively 'heavy' force.

In the latter half of 1941, Bomber Command suffered increasingly heavy losses. The exceptionally harsh winter that followed was doubtless to blame for some of these casualties, but when on 7 November 1941 thirty-seven aircraft failed to return from a force of 392 despatched, with Berlin as the main target, Churchill ordered that bombing operations be suspended until the following spring. In some respects, this gave the Command a welcome respite, with time to regroup and reassess the direction of the bomber offensive, but it also served to show it up to its critics in the Admiralty and the War Office as being a bottomless pit into which considerable resources had been thrown, to little effect.

However, it was not all doom and gloom for Bomber Command in 1941. The first of the new generation of four-engine bomber aircraft destined to transform its striking power began to come on stream with frontline squadrons, beginning in February with the Short Stirling, swiftly followed in March by the Handley Page Halifax, and by the superlative Avro Lancaster in March 1942. The trio of new heavies gradually replaced the obsolescent twin-engine Wellingtons, Whitleys and Hampdens that had so valiantly borne the brunt of the early offensive.

On 22 February 1942 Bomber Command and the bomber offensive gathered fresh momentum with the appointment of a new and dynamic commander-in-chief, Air Chief Marshal Sir Arthur Harris. Known to his crews as 'Butch', he immediately set about stifling criticism from his detractors by launching the first 1,000-bomber raid in May the same year, against Cologne, which simultaneously proved to the Germans and some opponents nearer to home in Whitehall that Bomber Command meant business and was far from being a spent force.

During 1942 three scientific research projects began to reach fruition,

Below: The Butt Report in August 1941 revealed to RAF commanders that few if any of Bomber Command's night bomber aircraft reached their targets, let alone dropped their bombs anywhere near them.
(IWM CH11542)

enabling Bomber Command to radically improve its navigation and bombing accuracy. These were Gee, which first saw use in February 1942, followed later that year in December by Oboe, and in January 1943 by H2S.

Without doubt, 1943 was a watershed for the fortunes of Bomber Command. At this mid-point in the war it possessed a heavy bomber force made up almost exclusively of four-engine aircraft, flown by better-trained crews using the latest in radar technology for navigation and target finding, and guided over land and sea by Pathfinders, enabling them to drop their bombs fairly and squarely on target, thanks to accurate target marking, improved bombsights and better bombs.

Not all Bomber Command's war efforts were channelled into mass attacks on urban targets. A number of high-profile precision raids on key targets were flown both in daylight and at night by small forces of heavy bomber aircraft. The first deep penetration daylight raid by a small force of Lancasters was mounted against the MAN diesel engine factory at Augsburg on 17 April 1942. Seven of the twelve attacking

Below: Locating a target in daylight and from low level did not pose the same problems for the light bomber squadrons of 2 Group, but the danger from flak and fighters was probably greater. Here, smoke rises from the Matford truck factory at Poissy, 10 miles from Paris, following an unescorted daylight attack by Boston medium bombers of 88 and 226 Squadrons on 8 March 1942. (IWM C2202)

Left: Following his appointment as Commander-in-Chief in February 1942, Air Chief Marshal Sir Arthur Harris – architect of the RAF's strategic bomber offensive – set Bomber Command firmly on course to becoming a powerful and effective weapon of war.
(*Crown Copyright*)

Below: Bomber Command's trio of four-engine heavy bombers transformed the RAF's striking capability. The Handley Page Halifax entered service in February 1942. This example, a B Mk V, is undergoing servicing at an airfield in Yorkshire.
(*IWM CH14222*)

The first four-engine heavy bomber into service was the Short Stirling in August 1910. These are Stirlings of 1651 Heavy Conversion Unit.

(Rover Group 9955)

aircraft were lost and the attack proved a costly failure, reinforcing the fact that in daylight unescorted bomber aircraft were easy prey for enemy fighters. High-risk raids such as this incurred the ire of Bomber Harris, who was vociferous in his condemnation of attacks on so-called panacea targets that were supposed to shorten the war.

Perhaps the most widely known precision bombing attack of the war was that on the Ruhr dams on 16–17 May 1943 by a force of nineteen specially modified Lancasters of 617 Squadron led by W/C Guy Gibson. With its risky combination of an untried miracle weapon and panacea targets, the plans for Operation Chastise would have been vetoed by Harris and the Air Ministry had it not been for the dogged persistence of Barnes Wallis, the vision of a handful of influential government scientists and the backing of the Chief of the Air Staff. The story of the planning, execution and aftermath of this epic operation is the subject of this book.

The third and most successful of Bomber Command's trio of four-engine heavy bombers to enter service was the Avro Lancaster, in March 1942. Here, 57 Squadron Lancasters are seen at Scampton in February 1943.
(IWM CH8785)

THE AEROPLANE
NOV. 5, 1943

The **LANCASTER**

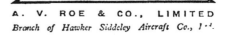

AVRO

A. V. ROE & CO., LIMITED
Branch of Hawker Siddeley Aircraft Co., Ltd.

CHAPTER 2

THE IMPOSSIBLE DREAM

DEVELOPING THE BOUNCING BOMB

For some years before the Second World War, the Air Ministry had harboured an interest in the possibility of attacking the large dams in Germany that fed the factories of the Ruhr. By 1937 a list of dams that were considered to be of strategic importance was drawn up, and in the following year the Air Ministry established a Bombing Committee to investigate the possibilities. With the likelihood of another world war looming, a meeting of the Committee on 26 July 1938 concluded that a low-level aerial attack against the German reservoir dams was feasible and should be examined further.

It was no secret to Britain's military planners that the heavy industry, domestic water supplies and river navigation of Germany's industrial heartland in the Ruhr Valley depended to a large degree on water storage in the upper reaches of the River Ruhr. During the Second World War a mighty stream of weapons and munitions flowed from its many factories and foundries to feed Germany's armed forces and the battlefronts on which they were engaged, from Norway to North Africa, and from the Atlantic Wall to the Russian Front.

Germany's reservoirs provided flood protection and during periods of drought guaranteed a minimum water flow in the rivers they fed. They also provided water supplies for industry and generated hydro-electricity. The two most important reservoirs were identified by the Air Ministry as being on tributaries of the River Ruhr – the Möhne and the Sorpe, with the Möhne reservoir providing more than a quarter of the storage capacity of all the reservoirs along the Ruhr. A third reservoir was on the River Eder, a tributary of the River Fulda, which flows

Above: A pre-war photograph of the Möhne dam. The power station that can be seen on the right of the picture was destroyed in the raid of 16–17 May 1943.

(Crown Copyright)

northwards as the River Weser and passes through the industrial city of Kassel. At that time, the Möhne and Sorpe dams provided 75 per cent of the Ruhr's water requirements. If they could be destroyed it would have a catastrophic effect upon German industry, not to mention morale.

When the Möhne dam was opened in 1913 it was one of the largest in Europe. Its elegantly curved 2,133ft-long wall made out of granite masonry blocks employed the latest in construction techniques to hold back 176 million cubic yards of water. Some 43 miles to the south-east of the Möhne lies the Eder dam, which was opened in 1914. Although its wall is 820ft shorter than the Möhne, it is still the largest reservoir in Germany and holds back 264 million cubic yards of water in a lake more than 16 miles long. Nine miles south-west of the Möhne is the Sorpe dam. Opened in 1935, the straight 2,297ft-long Sorpe was for many years Germany's highest earthen dam at 226ft high, and was constructed with an earth embankment around an inner concrete core.

The Möhne and Sorpe dams supplied water for the heavily industrialised Ruhr conurbation, and supply was mainly provided by the extraction of water from the River Ruhr. Owing to the natural flow characteristics of the river and the water loss to adjacent river basins, the continual demand for water in the Ruhr Valley could only be met by the operation of reservoirs on the tributaries of the River Ruhr. These reservoirs stored water during times of high water flow and discharged extra water during times of low natural flow. The highest flow at these dams was in March, when the reservoirs held back some 176 million cubic yards and 94 million cubic yards of water respectively.

Water was discharged from the Möhne and Sorpe reservoirs during the course of normal operations and was harnessed to produce hydro-electricity in power stations just below the dams. The amount of water discharged depended on water level requirements in the river below. However, the generation of hydro-electricity at both the Möhne and Sorpe dams was a by-product of the principal purpose of water quantity management. From the main power station, the water flowed into the compensating basin from which it was steadily discharged into the Möhne River via a secondary power station.

In breaching the Möhne dam alone, it was anticipated that a disaster of almost biblical proportions would be unleashed on the low-lying districts of the narrow Ruhr Valley. Large loss of life would be inevitable due to flooding, and industry would be seriously affected by restrictions on its supplies of water. Damage to the transport infrastructure of the region, such as roads, railways, and navigation on the River Ruhr, was also likely.

Between the Möhne dam and the city of Mulheim there were thirteen hydro-electricity generating stations, which would either be completely destroyed by the raging floodwaters, or have their energy production severely disrupted by wild fluctuations in water flow from the reservoir. Heavy industry in the Ruhr Valley – the blast furnaces, iron foundries and coke ovens – would be massively inconvenienced by a shortage of the water that was the lifeblood of their manufacturing processes.

The functions of the Eder dam were unrelated to those of the Möhne and Sorpe, and its primary purpose was flood prevention in the Hessen region. However, to release its 264 million cubic yards of water into the Eder, Fulda and Weser valleys would result in widespread flooding of large tracts of agricultural land and the possible inundation of the low-lying districts of the city of Kassel. The Mittelland Canal also relied upon a water supply from the Eder dam, that was pumped from the River Weser to maintain its levels. Added to this was the almost certain destruction of the four power stations situated in the shadow of the dam, which would have an effect on the operation of the Preussenelektra electricity supply system. On balance, however, it was believed that the effects of breaching the Eder dam would not be so devastating as those resulting from the destruction of the Möhne and Sorpe dams.

The Air Ministry planners realised that, to be effective, any attack on the great dams of western Germany would need to be mounted during the spring, when the water flow was at its greatest. Experience had

Aircraft of the RAF's bomber force in the early years of the Second World War were incapable of lifting, let alone accommodating large bombs. Here, in July 1940, armourers at Scampton prepare to bomb-up this Handley Page Hampden of 49 Squadron with 250lb and 500lb GP bombs. The heaviest weapon it could carry was a pair of slender 2,000lb SAP bombs. Clearly, lifting a 10-ton bomb was out of the question.

(IWM CH272)

THE RUHR DAMS, 1943

Möhne dam (Target X)
Length: 2,133ft
Height: 132ft max
Storage capacity: 176 million cu yds

Sorpe dam (Target Z)
Length: 2,297ft
Height: 226ft
Storage capacity: 94 million cu yds

Lister dam (Target D)
Length: 866ft
Height: 131ft
Storage capacity: 29 million cu yds

Ennepe dam (Target E)
Length: 1,083ft
Height: 165ft
Storage capacity: 20 million cu yds

Eder dam (Target Y)
Length: 1,309ft
Height: 139ft
Storage capacity: 264 million cu yds

Diemel dam (Target F)
Length: 637ft
Height: 131ft
Storage capacity: 26 million cu yds

COMPARISONS WITH DAMS AROUND THE WORLD

Hoover dam, USA
Length: 1,244ft
Height: 736ft
Storage capacity: 46 million cu yds

Kariba dam, Zimbabwe
Length: 1,900ft
Height: 420ft
Storage capacity: 235 billion cu yds

shown that narrow structures like dam walls presented very difficult targets to hit when seen from overhead. They were also resistant to destruction from conventional bombing attacks. Thus, the challenge that now faced the planners was how to mount a successful attack when the RAF's existing bomber aircraft, arsenal of bombs, and tactics were clearly not up to the task.

When the Second World War broke out on 3 September 1939, 52-year-old Barnes Wallis was employed as the Assistant Chief Designer of Vickers-Armstrong's Aviation Section at Weybridge in Surrey. Guy Gibson was later to describe him in his book *Enemy Coast Ahead* as 'neither young nor old, but just a quiet, earnest man who worked very hard. He was one of the real back room boys . . .'. As an aeronautical engineer, his reputation was already second to none through the design of the R100 airship and the Wellesley and Wellington bombers. On 4 September 1940, when the Battle of Britain was at its height, the Luftwaffe bombed the Vickers factory at Weybridge. Severe casualties and major damage resulted, and Wallis and his design staff were hurriedly evacuated to requisitioned offices in the grand setting of nearby Burhill Golf Club at Hersham, near Walton-on-Thames. At this time, and quite independent of the Air Ministry's deliberations on the subject, it became apparent that Wallis had been working for several months on a number of projects to design air-launched weapons capable of destroying supposedly invulnerable structures, of which the Ruhr dams were high on his list.

Wallis considered the design of bombs currently in use by the RAF and concluded that a 10-ton bomb shaped like a teardrop and dropped into a reservoir within 150ft of a dam wall would have a good chance of fatally damaging the structure. Tests were conducted at the National Physical Laboratory (NPL) in Teddington

Above: Barnes Wallis, inventor of the bouncing bomb, pictured after the war.
(Vickers)

using a wind tunnel model to determine the likely performance of the new bomb.

Because the RAF's existing bomber force was quite incapable of lifting a 10-ton bomb, Wallis also turned his mind to designing a high-altitude six-engined stratospheric bomber, named 'Victory', to carry the proposed huge weapon. With the encouragement of Vickers, in July 1940 he had attempted to persuade the Air Ministry to approve the development of this ambitious new aircraft. Disappointingly for Wallis, his enthusiasm was not shared by ministers and officials at Adastral House and 'Victory' never got beyond the drawing board. However, the Air Ministry did acknowledge the need for high-altitude aircraft and large bombs, and requested Vickers to speed up the development of existing aircraft designs to meet these requirements.

Meanwhile, a different set of tests was commenced at the Road Research Laboratory (RRL) in Harmondsworth, under the supervision of its director, Dr William Glanville. With the outbreak of war in 1939, the resources of the Department of Scientific and Industrial Research (DSIR) had been reorganised and the RRL became the principal centre for research on civil defence matters. However, as the war gathered pace, it became increasingly involved in military projects. In October 1940 Glanville formed a small research team headed by engineer A.R. Collins to carry out tests that investigated possibilities for

destroying dams. Wallis
visited the RRL at this time to discuss plans
for the tests with Glanville, Collins and Dr A.H.
Davis (Assistant Director of the RRL). He
suggested the three main targets should be the
Möhne and Eder masonry gravity dams in Germany and the Santa
Chiara di Ula multiple-arch dam in Sardinia. (The latter was never
attacked even though it was the most vulnerable.)

Also in October, the first in a series of trials was carried out on a
roughly built 1/50th-scale model of the Möhne dam to determine
whether a big bomb could destroy it. A gravity dam relied on its own
weight for stability, and the accuracy of the model test could not be
relied upon because it was impossible to scale down the effects of
gravity, even though all the dimensions, materials and explosive charges

Only when the Avro Lancaster entered RAF
service in 1942 did Bomber Command come into
possession of a potent bomber aircraft that, with
modification, was capable of lifting Wallis's 10-ton
bomb. This Lancaster served with two frontline
squadrons before relegation to a training unit in
1944.

(Author's collection)

Above: A 1/50th scale model of the Möhne dam was painstakingly constructed at the Building Research Station at Garston, near Watford, for experimental purposes. Test charges were exploded close to the inner wall to see what it would take before the structure failed.

(TRL Ltd)

used in the model and the test were accurately scaled down from the full size. The results were not encouraging, and by May 1941 the Air Staff had abandoned Wallis's idea for a big bomb, at least for the time being. However, the RRL continued testing.

Meanwhile, between November 1940 and January 1941, further tests were carried out at the Building Research Station at Garston, near Watford, on a more precisely constructed 1/50th-scale model of the Möhne dam. A series of ten test explosions was carried out using 2oz charges at a distance of between one and three feet from the dam wall; but the structure held. The tests were later moved to Harmondsworth, where further trials were undertaken.

Although his initial ideas had failed to find favour, when Wallis approached Dr D.R. Pye, the Director of Scientific Research (DSR) at the Ministry of Aircraft Production (MAP), with his latest theory, he found a receptive mind. Pye sanctioned use of the Road Research Laboratory for a trials programme to assess the effects of explosive charges when placed against or near the wall of a gravity-type dam. An informal committee (the Aerial Attack on Dams Committee) was formed on 10 March to monitor progress and coordinate any developments that came out of the trials.

In the same month Wallis began to examine the destructive characteristics of a bomb, and concluded that the pressure or shock waves occurring in air, earth or water could cause a structure to crack so severely that it would collapse completely. It was widely accepted that gravity dams like the Möhne and Eder, together with earth types like the Sorpe, were particularly difficult structures to breach. The first two were enormous concrete or masonry structures set on a broad base and with a high wall, triangular in cross-section to give strength. The latter, constructed of two sloping earth and rubble banks encasing a vertical concrete core, was almost invulnerable to direct hits from bombs or the effects of shock waves. However, in all cases, if the dam wall could be fractured by shock waves from an underwater explosion, then there was a strong possibility that the whole structure would fail due to the huge back-pressure of water in the reservoir. The big question was how could an explosive charge be placed against the inner face of a dam, a charge powerful enough to cause the complete failure of a gravity dam and cause serious leakage in an earth dam?

Further trials involving another 1/50th-scale model of the Möhne dam and the full-size Nant-y-Gro dam in mid-Wales were to prove that the Möhne dam could be breached if 6,500lb of high explosive could be detonated against the inner wall of the dam.

The disused Nant-y-Gro dam was a small structure built out of mass concrete and measured 180ft long. It was straight in plan and had been built across a stream in the beautiful Elan Valley, near Rhayader, to create a one-million-gallon reservoir. Situated as it was in a remote corner of Wales, Nant-y-Gro was ideally placed for the top-secret trials to take place. On 1 May 1942, the first live explosive tests were carried out on the dam, but they did not seriously damage the structure. After further development work, another attempt was made in July of that year when an explosive charge was suspended from the mid-point of the dam at the optimum depth, and detonated remotely. The result was a success: a huge central section of the dam wall, measuring 60ft wide by 24ft deep, was successfully breached.

A key factor in the success of this venture was to ensure that the explosive charge was placed flush against the dam wall. The tests had established that multiple-arch and gravity dams could be successfully breached, but only with a direct hit on the water face of a gravity dam

Below: The redundant Nant-y-Gro dam near Rhayader in mid-Wales was earmarked as a likely guinea pig for a series of explosives trials against a full-size dam structure. Beforehand, however, a scale model (seen here) was built to test calculations. *(TRL Ltd)*

Above: The real thing: an explosive charge is detonated against the inside wall of the Nant-y-Gro dam in Wales, throwing a huge column of water over the parapet.

(TRL Ltd)

Main picture: Special measuring equipment was used to gauge the efficacy of the scaled-down explosive charges used against the dam wall.

(TRL Ltd)

Far right: Nant-y-Gro, 2001. The swathe of pine trees marks the location of the dam wall (in the foreground) and its reservoir.

(Author)

POINT OF RELEASE - APPROX 400-450 YDS UPSTREAM

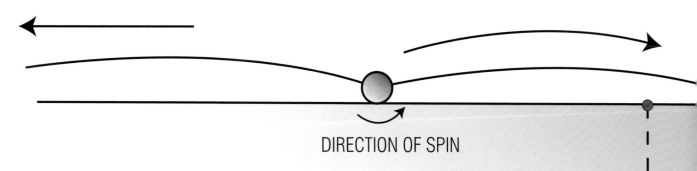

DIRECTION OF SPIN

TORPEDO NETTING BOOMS

Above: This diagram explains how Barnes Wallis's revolutionary bomb was designed to bounce across the surface of the water, skipping anti-torpedo nets, before striking the inner face of the dam wall and sliding beneath the water to a predetermined depth before exploding and breaching the structure.

(Bow Watkinson)

at a specified depth with a single charge of explosive weighing between 7,000 and 9,000lb. A charge that was detonated 50ft from the wall would need some 30,000lb of high explosive, a requirement clearly beyond the capabilities of the RAF at that time – but a 9,000lb bomb was within the carrying capacity of current aircraft such as the new four-engine Avro Lancaster. The biggest problem lay in achieving the precision of bomb-aiming.

So, how could the smaller quantity of explosive be planted right up against the inner wall of the dam? Wallis set his mind to the problem. In April 1942 he began working on a proposal for a spherical bomb

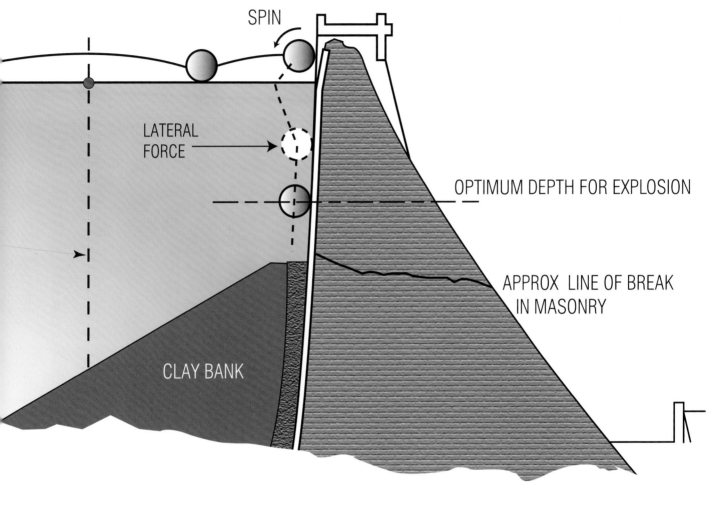

that could be mechanically back-spun by the launching aircraft and
released from low level about 400–500yds from the dam face. It would
then bounce across the surface of the reservoir until it reached the dam
wall and sink to a depth of 30ft, where it would explode. The back-
spinning – similar to skimming a flat stone on water in the game 'ducks
and drakes' – was important to increase the effective speed and range
of the weapon and to ensure that it would rebound when it hit the dam
wall and crawl down the inner face before detonating.

In mid-May, Wallis's paper was read by his friend Professor P.M.S.
Blackett, Scientific Adviser to the board of the Admiralty and a leading

Above: The 640ft-long No. 2 Ship Tank at the National Physical Laboratory (NPL), Teddington, which was used by Barnes Wallis to perfect delivery of the spherical weapon that eventually became the bouncing bomb. A selection of spheres the size of cricket balls simulating a full-size weapon were fired from a specially constructed catapult fitted to the gantry over the tank, which can be seen in the background of this photograph. Along with the other water tanks at the NPL, No. 2 Ship Tank was demolished in 1998.

(*HMSO/National Physical Laboratory*)

experimental physicist, who was impressed enough to pass it on to Sir Henry Tizard, Scientific Adviser to the Chief of the Air Staff. Tizard shared Blackett's enthusiasm, and in early June he authorised use of the Shipping Research Tanks at the NPL in Teddington for further trials. When top brass from the Air Ministry, Admiralty and MAP attended a demonstration of the mine at Teddington on 21 June 1942 they were so impressed by its potential that they immediately sanctioned full-scale live trials.

A number of twin-engine Vickers Wellington bombers were specially modified for aerial trials and six half-size inert prototype spherical mines were built for experimental purposes, fabricated from steel in several different configurations – ribbed, smooth and wooden-clad. Two mines at a time were carried in tandem inside the open bomb bay and back-spun before they were dropped. On 3 December 1942 Captain Joe 'Mutt' Summers, the Vickers chief test pilot, flew Wellington Mk II, BJ895, from the Dorset fighter airfield at Warmwell for the first test drop of the mine off Chesil Beach on the Dorset coast. Lying on the bomb-aimer's couch in the nose of the 'Wimpy' was Barnes Wallis who, when the time came, pressed the tit and released the mine. Unfortunately, the results were not good because the mines shattered on contact with the water, but a further test flight was conducted on the 15th and the trials continued. On 5 February 1943 the weapon finally proved itself when solid wood mines achieved the desired results and the bouncing bomb, now code-named 'Upkeep', finally became a reality. It was not until late in April that the size and shape of the weapon was finally decided upon.

When the Controller of Research and Development (CRD) at the MAP passed the results to the Air Staff, he cautioned that producing a full-size operational version of the bomb in time to bomb the Ruhr dams in May 1943, when the water levels were at their highest, was out of the question. Instead, he suggested delaying use until the trials of the 'Highball' ship-busting weapon were completed. In any case, there was a danger that secrecy and surprise could be compromised on the parallel development of this spherical weapon if Upkeep went ahead.

It was at this point that Upkeep came close to being abandoned, after Wallis had encountered stiff resistance to his invention from Lord Cherwell, the CRD and the Commander-in-Chief of Bomber Command, Sir Arthur Harris. It took the personal intervention of Sir Charles Portal, Chief of the Air Staff, to save the day. He overruled their concerns and decreed that the project should go ahead with the utmost urgency. On 26 February, orders were issued for the immediate conversion of three Avro Lancaster bombers for operational trials, a

Below: Several specially modified Wellington bombers were used to conduct trials using inert prototype spherical mines. The earliest trials with the dummy weapons were carried out between 4 and 15 December 1942 by Wellington Mk II, BJ895, flown by Vickers' chief test pilot, Mutt Summers, with Barnes Wallis as bomb aimer. Two prototype spherical mines can here be seen in the converted bomb bay.
(Vickers)

Above: Captain Joseph 'Mutt' Summers, chief test pilot at Vickers-Armstrongs, played an important part in the trials of the bouncing bomb.
(*Vickers*)

Main picture: Further trials took place in December 1942 and January 1943 in the sea off Chesil Beach in Dorset. The initial results were not promising, but on 23 January the bouncing bomb theory was at last proved credible. The size and cylindrical shape of the bomb was finally confirmed in late April.
(*IWM FLM2368*)

Far right: R.C. (Bob) Handasyde was also closely involved as a flight test observer in the trials.
(*Vickers*)

'UPKEEP' BOUNCING BOMB

Type: cylindrical air dropped mine

Total weight: 9,250lb (4,195kg)

Dimensions – diameter: 50in (125cm); length: 60in (150cm)

Explosive charge: 6,600lb (2,995kg) Torpex – (41.7% Trinitrotoluol, 40.5% Hexogen, 17.5% aluminium

Detonators: three Mk XIV hydrostatic pistols each containing a primer charge of Tetryl to activate at a depth of 30ft (9m)

Self-destruct pistol: one

Optimum rotation speed: 500rpm back-spun

Delivery height and speed: 60ft at 210–220mph

---

further twenty for conversion for operational use, and 150 bombs.

Vickers-Armstrongs at Barrow were contracted to manufacture the Upkeep mines, and Vickers also made the bomb-carrying and release mechanisms. Modification of the Lancasters was jointly undertaken by Avro and Vickers, with the latter using facilities at RAE Farnborough. Such was the urgency of the task that both contractors worked round-the-clock shifts, seven days a week.

The Upkeep bomb itself was in fact not a bomb but a cylindrical aerial mine, although it was invariably referred to as a bouncing bomb. Made out of metal some 3/8th inch thick, it measured about 60 inches in length by 50 inches in diameter and contained 6,600lb of Torpex explosive. Three hydrostatic pistols were set to detonate the explosive charge at a depth of 30ft and a fourth self-destruct pistol was timed to go off 90 seconds after the bomb had been released. Upkeep weighed in

Above: Cut-away illustration of the dam-busting weapon showing the three hydrostatic pistol detonators.

at 9,250lb and was carried in the belly of the specially modified Lancaster from which the bomb doors and mid-upper gun turret had been removed. Carried in the aperture that had been the bomb bay, the bomb was mounted between two side-swing calliper arms, each of which was fitted with a 20in diameter disc. These corresponded to two circular tracks, one on each end of the cylindrical bomb, the back-spin being transmitted by friction generated between the driven discs and the circular tracks. Power for rotation was supplied by a Vickers Jassey Variable Speed Gear hydraulic motor driving a belt at an angle of 45 degrees, running in a groove on the driven disc in the starboard calliper arm. Hydraulic power originally intended for the Lancaster's mid-upper turret and the bomb bay doors was diverted to the hydraulic motor that was mounted in the floor of the fuselage in the facing of the bomb bay.

From his position just forward of the main spar, the wireless operator switched on the hydraulic motor that spun the bomb and he adjusted its rotation speed to the required 500rpm. Up in the cockpit beyond the navigator's curtained-off compartment, the pilot concentrated on flying straight and level while the flight engineer controlled the speed of the Lancaster on the approach run to the dam,

Below: In February 1943 the Chief of the Air Staff, Sir Charles Portal, ordered the immediate conversion of three Lancaster bombers for operational trials of 'Upkeep', as the bouncing bomb was now code-named.

This view from beneath the Lancaster's nose, looking aft, shows the mine in place and protruding from the converted bomb bay.

(Crown Copyright)

This well-known view of Guy Gibson's Lancaster, ED932/AJ-G, clearly shows the cut-away bomb bay with the Upkeep weapon mounted between the pair of side-swing callipers, and the belt drive to the weapon.

(*Crown Copyright*)

FORWARD

VSG. HYDRAULIC
MOTOR
MOUNTED ON A
WOODEN BLOCK

SPRING TENSION
NUT.

SUPPORTING TRUSS

FUSING UNIT

TRUSSES SWING
OUTWARDS TO
RELEASE BOMB

LANYARD FOR ARMING
HYDROSTATIC PISTOL

17" PULLEY

DIRECTION OF
ROTATION

BOMB BAY
ROOF STRUCTURE

HINGE

Detail drawing of the bouncing bomb installation.
(D.H. Cooksey/Aero Modeller)

Ⓐ

TIE ROD AND SPRING
UNDER COMPRESSION.

FREE SPINNER

12000 LBS BOMB SLIP
RELEASES FOUR
TIE RODS.

Ⓐ DETAIL OF RELEASE UNIT

ORES
50 LBS.

Above: ED817/AJ-C flew on the Upkeep dropping trials at Reculver on 20 April 1943. Note the cut-away bomb bay and absence of dorsal turret.
(Bruce Robertson collection)

Below: Illustration of the Type 464 Provisioning modifications made to the Lancaster in order for it to carry Upkeep.
(Bruce Robertson collection)

and the navigator switched on the twin spotlights mounted on the underside of the aircraft. Looking out of the Perspex blister on the starboard side of the cockpit canopy, the navigator instructed the pilot on the necessary height corrections until the desired figure-of-eight alignment of the spotlights on the water below had been achieved.

When the bomb-aimer pressed the bomb-release button, powerful springs caused the calliper arms to spring outwards, thereby allowing the mine to drop free from the aircraft while at the same time arming the hydrostatic pistols.

The accurate delivery of Upkeep onto the target sounded difficult enough on paper, and the rigorous flying training programme devised for 617 Squadron's aircrews only served to emphasise this point. In fact, it became probably the longest, most intensive and most arduous bombing mission practice of the entire war.

CHAPTER 3

TRAINING FOR THE DAMS

Despite his vehement opposition to what he considered a crackpot invention by a mad scientist, Bomber Harris finally relented. On 15 March 1943 he ordered the formation of a special new bomber squadron. Harris's reluctant change of heart was due largely to pressure from the Chief of the Air Staff, Sir Charles Portal, who had been sufficiently impressed by the bomb trials at Chesil Beach and the model tests in the ship tanks at Teddington. Portal now wanted development of the bomb, modification of the aircraft and training of the Lancaster crews to proceed with the utmost urgency if the attack on the dams was to be mounted before the latest optimum date of 26 May. However, Harris warned Cochrane, the AOC of 5 Group, that the creation of the new squadron should not impact on the efforts of Bomber Command's Main Force squadrons, and that the planned attack on the Ruhr dams would not be its only task.

On 17 March the new squadron was officially formed. Known initially as Squadron X, it was to be commanded by a highly experienced 24-year-old wing commander named Guy Gibson. With two bomber and one night fighter tours under his belt already, and sporting the medal ribbons of two DSOs and two DFCs, Gibson had been the commanding officer of 106 Squadron at Syerston before his appointment to head up the new and top-secret Squadron X.

Bomber Command decreed that the crews for this new squadron were to be volunteers who had already completed at least one, and possibly two, bomber tours. Over the years a myth has grown up suggesting that all the men were young, highly experienced bomber veterans personally selected by Gibson. The reality is somewhat different, as the eminent aviation historian John Sweetman records in his book *The Dambusters Raid*: 'Not all the pilots were personally known to Gibson; aircrew ages ranged from twenty to thirty-two; the majority were not decorated (including six of the pilots); and far from having finished two operational tours some had not done one. Many who would fly to the German dams in May 1943 had completed fewer than ten operations against enemy targets, and some of the flight engineers were actually on their first.'

Squadron commander: W/C G.P. Gibson, DSO and Bar, DFC and Bar
Crew: Sgt J. Pulford DFM (FE), P/O T.H. Taerum DFC (Nav), F/L E.G. Hutchison DFC and Bar (W/Op), P/O F.M. Spafford DFC (BA), F/S G.A. Deering DFC, RCAF (FG), F/L R.A.D. Trevor-Roper DFC (RG)

F/L J.V. Hopgood DFC and Bar (Captain)
Crew: Sgt C. Brennan (FE), F/O K. Earnshaw RCAF (N), Sgt J.W. Minchin (W/Op), P/O J.W. Fraser DFM (BA), P/O G.H.F.G. Gregory DFM (FG), P/O A.F. Burcher DFM, RAAF (RG)

F/L H.B.M Martin DFC (Captain)
Crew: P/O I. Whittaker (FE), F/L J.F. Leggo DFC, RAAF (N), F/O L. Chambers RNZAF (W/Op), F/L R.C. Hay DFC, RAAF (BA), P/O T.B. Foxlee DFM, RAAF (FG), F/S T.D. Simpson RAAF (RG)

Gibson and S/L David Maltby, one of his flight commanders on 617 Squadron, pose for the camera in Gibson's office at Scampton. They are pictured after the dams raid on 22 July 1943. (IWM TR1122)

Centre: P/O Les Knight RAAF (AJ-N) with his 617 Squadron crew. From left to right: F/O H.S. Hobday RAFVR, F/O Edward Johnson RAFVR, Sgt Fred Sutherland RCAF, P/O Les Knight RAAF, P/O Bob Kellow RAAF, Sgt Ray Grayston RAFVR, Sgt Harry O'Brien RCAF.

(IWM CH11049)

S/L H.M. Young DFC and Bar (Captain)
Crew: Sgt D.T. Horsfall (FE), F/S C.W. Roberts (N), Sgt L.W. Nichols (W/Op), F/O V.S. MacCausland RCAF (BA), Sgt G.A. Yeo (FG), Sgt W. Ibbotson (RG)

F/L D.J. Maltby (Captain)
Crew: Sgt W. Hatton (FE), Sgt V. Nicholson (N), Sgt A.J.B. Stone (W/Op), P/O J. Fort (BA), Sgt V. Hill (FG), Sgt H.T. Simmonds (RG)

F/L D. Shannon DFC, RAAF (Captain)
Crew: Sgt R.J. Henderson (FE), F/O D.R. Walker DFC, RCAF (N), F/O B. Goodale DFC (W/Op), F/S L.J. Sumpter (BA), Sgt B. Jagger (FG), F/O J. Buckley (RG)

S/L H.E. Maudslay DFC (Captain)
Crew: Sgt J. Marriot (FE), F/O R.A. Urquhart (N), WO2 A.P. Cottam (W/Op), P/O M.J.D. Fuller (BA), F/O J. Tytherleigh (FG), Sgt N.R. Burrows (RG)

F/L W. Astell DFC (Captain)
Crew: Sgt J. Kinnear (FE), P/O F.A. Wile (N), WO2 A. Garshowitz (W/Op), F/O D. Hopkinson (BA), F/S F.A. Garbas (FG), Sgt R. Bolitho (RG)

P/O L.G. Knight RAAF (Captain)
Crew: Sgt R.E. Grayston (FE), F/O H.S. Hobday (N), F/S R.G.T. Kellow (W/Op), F/O E.C. Johnson (BA), Sgt F.E. Sutherland (FG), Sgt H.E. O'Brien (RG)

F/L R.N.G. Barlow DFC, RAAF (Captain)
Crew: P/O S.L. Whillis (FE), F/O P.S. Burgess (N), F/O C.R. Williams DFC, RAAF (W/Op), P/O A. Gillespie DFM (BA), F/O H.S. Glinz RCAF (FG), Sgt J.R.G. Liddell (RG)

F/L J.L. Munro (Captain)
Crew: Sgt F.E. Appleby (FE), F/O F.G. Rumbles (N), Sgt P.E. Pigeon (W/Op), Sgt J.H. Clay (BA), Sgt W. Howarth (FG), F/S H.A. Weeks (RG)

P/O V.W. Byers (Captain)
Crew: Sgt A.J. Taylor (FE), F/O J.H. Warner (N), Sgt J. Wilkinson (W/Op), P/O A.N. Whitaker (BA), Sgt C.McA. Jarvie (FG), F/S McDowell (RG)

P/O G. Rice (Captain)

Crew: Sgt E.C. Smith (FE), F/O R. MacFarlane (N), Sgt C.B. Gowrie (W/Op), F/S J.W. Thrasher (BA), Sgt T.W. Maynard (FG), Sgt S. Burns (RG)

F/L J.C. McCarthy (Captain)

Crew: Sgt W. Radcliffe (FE), F/S D.A. MacLean (N), Sgt L. Eaton (W/Op), Sgt G.L. Johnson (BA), Sgt R. Batson (FG), F/O D. Rodger (RG)

P/O W. Ottley (Captain)

Crew: Sgt R. Marsden (FE), F/O J.K. Barrett (N), Sgt J. Guterman (W/Op), F/S T.B. Johnston (BA), Sgt F. Tees (FG), Sgt H.J. Strange (RG)

P/O L.J. Burpee (Captain)

Crew: Sgt G.Pegler (FE), Sgt T. Jaye (N), P/O L.G.Weller (W/Op), WO2 J.L. Arthur (BA), Sgt W.C.A. Long (FG), WO2 J.G. Brady (RG)

F/S K.W. Brown (Captain)

Crew: Sgt H.B. Feneron (FE), Sgt D.P. Heal (N), Sgt H.J. Hewstone (W/Op), Sgt S. Oancia (BA), Sgt D. Allatson (FG), F/S G.S. MacDonald (RG)

P/O W.C. Townsend (Captain)

Crew: Sgt D.J.D. Powell (FE), P/O C.L. Howard (N), F/S A. Chalmers (W/Op), Sgt C.E. Franklin (BA), Sgt D.E. Webb (FG), Sgt R.Wilkinson (RG)

F/S C.T. Anderson (Captain)

Crew: Sgt R.C. Patterson (FE), Sgt J.P. Nugent (N), Sgt W.D. Bickle (W/Op), Sgt G.J. Green (BA), Sgt E. Ewan (FG), Sgt A.W. Buck (RG)

Key: FE = flight engineer; N = navigator; W/Op = wireless operator; BA = bomb aimer; FG = front gunner; RG = rear gunner

No. 106 Squadron provided three crew captains in F/L John Hopgood, 21, from Seaford in Sussex, along with 20-year-old F/L David Shannon DFC, RAAF, and F/S Lewis Burpee DFM, RCAF, aged 25, newly married and from Ottawa, Ontario.

Another 5 Group squadron, No. 57, provided three more pilots in the shape of P/O Geoff Rice, the 23-year-old Mancunian F/L Bill Astell

Overleaf: F/L David Shannon, pilot of AJ-L (left), with F/L Dick Trevor-Roper, Gibson's rear gunner on the dams raid, and S/L George Holden who was later to succeed Gibson as CO of 617 Squadron. *(IWM TR1129)*

DFC, and S/L Melvin 'Dinghy' Young DFC, who had sixty-five trips under his belt already. 'Dinghy' was so named because he had ditched twice in the North Sea. An Oxford rowing Blue, Young was Gibson's deputy as well as the commander of A Flight and was described by him as 'a big man, and a very efficient organiser. I was to find out later that he could drink a pint of beer faster than any other man I know.'

The B Flight commander was the ex-50 Squadron old-Etonian S/L Henry Maudslay DFC, 21 years of age, from the Cotswold village of Broadway in Worcestershire. Also from 50 Squadron were F/L Mick Martin DFC (a highly experienced Aussie pilot and an expert in low-level flying, serving in the RAF) and P/O Les Knight RAAF. In fact, 50 Squadron had been the breeding ground for some of the finest pilots and crews in Bomber Command, of which Guy Gibson and Mick Martin were among the three greatest bomber pilots of the Second World War.

No. 207 Squadron provided P/O Warner Ottley DFC, while 44 Squadron supplied 23-year-old F/S Ken Brown RCAF, from Moose Jaw, Saskatchewan. Also from Saskatchewan was P/O Vernon Byers RCAF, aged 32, from the town of Codette.

From 97 Squadron came F/L David Maltby DFC – 'large and thoughtful, a fine pilot'; F/L Les Munro RNZAF – 'a most charming fellow with an excellent operational record. He was one of those types who can always be relied on to do the right thing at the right moment.' And a 23-year-old American, F/L Joe McCarthy DFC, RCAF. Born in St James, Long Island, McCarthy grew up in Brooklyn but when war broke out in Europe in 1939 he was desperate to see some action and so joined the RCAF, coming over to Britain to fly with Bomber Command in 1942. From St Kilda, Australia, via 61 Squadron, came 32-year-old F/L Robert Barlow DFC, RAAF, and from 49 Squadron Sgt Cyril Anderson and Sgt Bill Townsend DFM.

Three other pilots were posted in to 617 Squadron, but did not fly on the dams raid. They were 28-year-old F/L Harold Wilson from Tottenham, north London, and P/O William Divall, 21, from Thornton Heath, Surrey (who had been brought in to replace Sgt Lovell and crew), both of whose crews were prevented from flying on Chastise due to sickness in their number. Later both captains were shot down by light flak and killed, as were their entire crews, as they attacked the Mittelland Canal on 15–16 September 1943. F/S G. Lanchester RCAF and his crew opted to leave the squadron after Gibson threatened to replace their navigator.

The 5 Group bomber airfield of Scampton in Lincolnshire was chosen as the base for Squadron X. Situated 5 miles north of the city of Lincoln, Gibson had been stationed there earlier in the war flying Hampdens when he was with 83 Squadron. The new aircrews began to arrive at Scampton on 21 March, while all non-flying personnel were on the base by 27 March. Squadron X officially became 617 Squadron on

The Derwent dam and reservoir in Derbyshire's Peak District was used to hone 617's low-flying and precision-bombing skills. Its twin towers were useful in testing the principle of the simple Dann bombsight that was specially invented for the purposes of Upkeep. Pictured here, on 16 May 1988, the BBMF's Lancaster overflies the Derwent dam to mark the 45th anniversary of the dams raid. For 6 miles around, more than 50,000 people thronged to witness the spectacle.

(Atlantic Syndication)

the 24th and its adjutant, F/L Harry Humphries, declared the new squadron ready to fly on the 25th.

On the 24th, Gibson travelled to see Barnes Wallis at Weybridge, where the scientist was hoping to give him a full briefing on the bomb and its intended targets. However, Gibson had not yet been cleared by Bomber Command to be given the full and specific details, so Wallis had to make do with outlining his ideas on the bomb and showing him a film of the bomb trials at Chesil Beach.

On the 27th, Cochrane's SASO, G/C Harry Satterly, remembered by Gibson as 'a big blunt man who had the habit of getting things done quickly and well', issued Gibson with written orders that outlined the reason for the new squadron's existence – well, almost. The specific details of their intended target were still withheld, although Satterly's orders described how 617 Squadron would be required to attack a number of lightly defended special targets, necessitating low-level navigation over enemy territory in moonlight with a final approach to the target at 100ft at a precise speed of 240mph. He went on to say that aircraft would be despatched at ten-minute intervals to attack Target A and upon its successful destruction all subsequent aircraft would be diverted en route to fly to Target B, Target C and so on until the objectives of the operation had been achieved. While still not giving the game away, Satterly advised Gibson to ensure see that his crews practised low-level flying over water, and on daylight training sorties to ensure that pilots and bomb aimers wore dark goggles to simulate moonlight conditions. To simulate night-flying conditions during daylight, blue celluloid was applied to the cockpit canopy and the gunners' turret Perspex, and amber-tinted interchangeable lenses were fitted to flying goggles. Helpfully, Satterly also told Gibson that there were nine lakes in Wales and the Midlands that were suitable for flying practice. That same day, 617 was ready to commence its intensive flying training programme using ten standard Lancasters borrowed from another squadron.

On the 28th, Gibson took off from Scampton in a Lancaster accompanied by F/L John Hopgood and S/L Melvin 'Dinghy' Young and headed for the Derwent reservoir and dam in Derbyshire's Peak District to practise low flying at the height outlined in Satterly's briefing. During the hours of daylight Gibson found this a relatively easy task, but when he attempted to do the same at dusk it became clear just how dangerous the job was going to be: 'With the fog already beginning to fill up in the valley, cutting visibility down to about a mile or so, we tried again. This time it wasn't so good. The water, which had been blue by day, was now black – we nearly hit that black water.' The next day Gibson was called to a meeting with Cochrane at 5 Group HQ in Grantham, where he was shown scale models of the Möhne and Sorpe dams and then told to visit Wallis again. It was on his next visit to Weybridge that Wallis and Mutt Summers explained to Gibson the construction of the Ruhr dams and their importance to German heavy industry.

Photo-reconnaissance of the dams was a vital ingredient to the success of Operation Chastise, as the attack on the dams was now code-named. It provided crucial information to Bomber Command's planning staff about the water levels in the dams' reservoirs as well as intelligence on anti-aircraft defences in the vicinity. Orders went out to RAF Benson in Oxfordshire on 25 January 1943 for one of its resident photo-reconnaissance units, 541 Squadron, to obtain coverage of the Möhne dam and its reservoir. On 7 February, the first in a series of nine PR sorties was flown to the Möhne by a Spitfire of 541 Squadron. The weather conditions over western Germany were not ideal for photography and it was not until the seventh attempt on the 19th that useful material was brought back. Two more sorties were deemed necessary to provide photographs of good enough quality to enable accurate scale models of the dam and its reservoir to be built for aircrew briefing purposes. Periodically, in the weeks that followed, the dam was photographed by 541 and 542 Squadrons to provide

Above: Squadron X became 617 Squadron on 24 March 1943, although its badge was not officially approved until several months later.

57

Above: One of the PRU's aims was to bring back photographs of high enough quality for skilled model makers to build three-dimensional scale models of the dams. This is a model of the Sorpe dam.
(IWM MH3780)

additional information about the dam itself and changes in the water level and defences.

On 5 April Bomber Command made a further request for photo-reconnaissance coverage, only this time to include the Eder and Sorpe dams. The final reconnaissance was completed by 15 May and the latest photographs and interpretations were ready by mid-afternoon that same day. Detailed scale models were built of both dams and their hinterlands to aid crews at their operational briefing. For the most part, photographic sorties to the dams were flown by the same pilots each time. This was to familiarise them with the dams and their surrounding landscapes, so that when they flew the post-raid reconnaissance sorties they would be able to accurately observe the changes brought about by the flooding.

Throughout April, when weather conditions permitted, the crews of 617 Squadron carried out intensive flying training on a daily basis, and by the end of that month Gibson was able to report that all his crews could navigate at low level by night, fly safely over water at a height of 150ft and bomb accurately with the aid of a special bombsight. In *Enemy Coast Ahead*, he remarked:

The boys had begun to get good at their flying, and now I knew where and what the targets were we could plan a route similar to the one which would actually be used over Germany. This meant flying a lot over lakes, but the excuse was always the same: they were good landmarks and a good check on navigation. As we would have to fly to Germany at tree-level height, keeping to track was most important, and it meant navigation to the yard.

From 5 May, all training was undertaken at the Eyebrook reservoir (also referred to as Uppingham Lake), where ten Lancasters at a time were to practise flying at 60ft above the water. In addition to this, cross-country flying exercises were still undertaken to further improve navigational skills that would prove invaluable when it came to the real operation. The Abberton reservoir near Colchester (also known as Colchester Lake) and Lake Bala in North Wales were also used for low-level flying and bombing practice.

In the days that followed, the skills of 617's nineteen bomber crews were honed to a high degree of operational capability – pilots could fly at 60ft over water while maintaining an air speed of 210mph; with the aid of Gee and careful map reading, navigators could find their way around the countryside with precision at low level in the dark; bomb-aimers had refined their techniques with practice bombs to achieve an average error of 117ft; and gunners had harmonised their sights and sharpened their gunnery skills to make them potent adversaries for enemy night fighters and flak gunners.

The crews themselves might have been trained and ready, but two important technical matters could make or break all their hard work – an effective bombsight with which to accurately aim the bombs, and a means of precisely calculating the height of an aircraft above the reservoirs.

First of all, because of the extreme low level at which the bombs were to be dropped, no bombsight then in use by the RAF could do the job. Surprisingly, the solution was very simple and effective. A hand-held wooden sight was designed by W/C C.L. Dann at the A&AEE

Below: These models were of vital importance for aircrew briefing purposes and were used in the final briefings at Scampton on 16 May 1943. Here is the Möhne dam. *(IWM MH842)*

Boscombe Down, for use by the bomb aimers of 617 Squadron. In order to achieve an accurate release point for the Upkeep weapon, Dann used calculations based on the width between the sluice towers of the Möhne dam to make a simple triangular wooden sight. With a sighting peephole at the apex and two nails at the extremities of the base, the bomb aimer held the sight by a wooden handle attached to the underside of the apex and looked through the peephole. On the bombing run, when the twin towers of the dam coincided with the two nails the bomb aimer pressed the bomb release mechanism. A trial flight over the Derwent dam proved the effectiveness of the device and Barnes Wallis worked out the relevant sighting data for each dam to be attacked.

However, the Dann sight had its drawbacks. Buffeting of the aircraft at low level by thermals meant that it was nearly impossible for a bomb aimer to hold a sight steady with both hands and still maintain his balance in the bomb-aiming compartment. Some bomb aimers dispensed with the Dann sight altogether and experimented with their own sighting devices, which included chinagraph pencil marks on the clear vision panel and lengths of string attached to screws each side of the panel to create a large triangle. Lying prone on the floor of the aircraft supported by their forearms, some bomb aimers saw this as a more stable position to adopt during the bombing run.

The conundrum of how to maintain a specific height at low level over water and in the dark taxed the greatest brains at the MAP and at RAE Farnborough. Gibson was at a loss to find an effective way of judging the right height, and in the end it was the gentle, kindly figure of Ben Lockspeiser, civilian Director of Scientific Research at MAP, who solved the riddle. Trials carried out in 1942 on Lockheed Hudsons of Coastal Command had used twin spotlights to assist in night attacks

Below: A scale model of the Eder dam.
(IWM MH27710)

on submarines in shallow water, but without success – the twin lights had converged *beneath* the rough surface of the water. Lockspeiser successfully argued that on the calm water of an inland lake this would not be a problem, and trials were quickly set up at Farnborough. After a series of tests it was decided that the optimum positioning for the twin Aldis lamps on a Lancaster would be one in the portside of the nose, aft of the bomb aimer's clear vision panel, and the second in the rear of the bomb bay. Both lamps were angled to starboard and when the aircraft was flying at the prescribed 150ft (later reduced to 60ft) above the water, the twin beams would converge to form a figure of eight on the water beneath and just forward of the leading edge of the starboard wing. This enabled the navigator to check the height from the Perspex blister on the starboard side of the cockpit.

It was not until 8 April that the first of the modified Lancasters reached the squadron. By the end of the month thirteen of the Type 464

Above: Standard RAF bombsights in 1943 were not sufficiently accurate to meet the low-level precision requirements for Upkeep. This is the Mk XIV Stabilised Vector Sight in a Lancaster. Introduced in 1942, and sometimes referred to as the 'area sight', by mid-1944 most operational heavy bomber aircraft in Bomber Command had been fitted with this bomb-aiming device. (IWM CH11542)

By early May, 617 Squadron had received 18 modified Type 464 Provisioning Lancasters. This is ED825 that was used at A&AEE Boscombe Down for handling trials of the fully loaded bomber. It was flown by F/L Joe McCarthy on Chastise. The side-swing calipers and drive belt can be clearly seen in this photograph.

(IWM ATP11384B)

A. V. ROE & CO., LIMITED

Avro Lancaster I (Type 464 Provisioning)

(Paul Couper)

Above: ED817 took part in the Upkeep dropping trials at Reculver on 20 April. Although the aircraft did not fly on the actual dams raid, this photograph gives a good indication of how much the bomb bay was re-modelled on the Type 464 Provisioning Lancasters.

(*Bruce Robertson collection*)

Above: Without its mid-upper turret and bomb bay doors, a modified Lancaster drops a full-size Upkeep in the sea on the north Kent coast at Reculver Bay during tests in May 1943. The first modified Lancasters reached 617 Squadron on 8 April and the Upkeep trials were switched from Chesil Beach to Reculver on the 13th because the latter offered better security and easier recovery of the dropped weapons for examination.

(IWM FLM2340)

AVRO LANCASTER B MK I (TYPE 464 PROVISIONING)

Power plant

Four Rolls-Royce Merlin 28 12-cylinder Vee liquid-cooled engines, rated at 1,460hp at 6,250ft in 'M' gear and 1,435hp at 11,000ft in 'S' gear

Performance

Maximum speed: 271mph at 6,250ft and 281mph at 11,000ft
Time to climb: 20,000ft in 41.6min
Service ceiling: 20,000ft (at max weight), 24,500ft (at mean weight)
Range with standard fuel and 10,000lb bomb load: 1,040 miles

Dimensions

Span: 102ft 0in ; *length:* 68ft 10in; *height:* 20ft 4in; *undercarriage track:* 23ft 9in; *wing area:* 1,300sq ft

Armament

Offensive: one 9,250lb cylindrical air-dropped 'Upkeep' mine
Defensive: two .303in machine guns in Frazer Nash FN5 hydraulically operated turret in nose; four .303in machine guns in FN20 rear turret; two .303in machine guns in FN64 ventral turret (not fitted for raid)

Provisioning aircraft had arrived, which meant that the borrowed unmodified Lancasters, used until then for training purposes, could be returned to their owner squadrons. However, because of the great haste in which the modifications had been carried out by the contractors, not everything had been completed on time. Therefore some of the modifications that should have been undertaken by Avro were carried out at Scampton by the base engineering staff, assisted by supervisors from Avro, RAE and MAP. By early May, eighteen modified Lancasters had been received and fitted with VHF radios; twenty Upkeep weapons had also been received and were ready for balancing (to ensure they rotated true and did not oscillate); practice Upkeeps had been delivered and were being prepared for crews to use in a night trial off Reculver on the North Kent coast.

On the night of 6/7 May, the squadron flew a full exercise over the Eyebrook, Abberton and Howden reservoirs, Derwent dam, Wainfleet and The Wash, simulating the attack pattern that had been planned for the actual operations against the Möhne, Eder and Sorpe dams. Three formations, each of three aircraft, carried out practice attacks on the reservoirs, and the Derwent dam, while the rest of the squadron, the mobile reserve, practised bombing over the Wash with the aid of their twin Aldis spotlights.

On 10 May Satterly wrote to G/C Charles Whitworth at Scampton

Below: People living near the isolated 4-mile-long Lake Bala in North Wales were frightened out of their wits as 617's Lancasters swept low over the lake at night on practice sorties.
(Author)

This page and opposite: This fascinating four-picture sequence shows a modified Lancaster making a trial drop of an Upkeep weapon. Flying at probably not more than 40ft above the sea, its rear fuselage and tail plane are engulfed by the great plume of water made by the bomb as it makes its first bounce. Although the Lancaster emerges largely intact, the tail plane appears to have suffered damage and it may have lost the tail wheel. ED921 flown by Les Munro, and ED933, flown by Henry Maudslay, were both damaged during the trials at Reculver due to flying below the prescribed height of 60ft. These important photographs are movie stills taken from a film that was only rediscovered in 1993, deep in the archives of TRL Ltd (formerly the Road Research Laboratory).

(IWM FLM 2360/1/2/3)

Above: In April 1975 four inert concrete-filled Upkeeps were recovered from the mud some 200yds offshore from Reculver. A USAF Sikorsky HH53 'Jolly Green Giant' helicopter was used to lift the bombs on to dry land.

with the first draft order for the forthcoming operation, which the station commander used as a discussion document with Gibson. It was resolved that the attack should be mounted by twenty Lancasters, with three sections of three aircraft taking off at ten-minute intervals, followed by individual aircraft taking off at three-minute intervals. Aircraft were to cross the North Sea at 60ft and maintain this low level across the continent, with the formation leader climbing to 500ft en route to check landmarks, and, when 10 miles from the target, climbing to between 1,000 and 1,500ft. Targets were designated A, B and C, corresponding to the Möhne, Eder and Sorpe dams. The leader would make an immediate assault on target A, and when he had completed his attack he would wait 90 seconds before calling in the second aircraft to attack, followed by the third. By this time the second formation would have arrived and the procedure would be repeated, with the third formation following on. Each aircraft would fire a red flare over the dam after dropping its mine as a safety precaution for the next aircraft in line to attack. When target A had been destroyed, aircraft would divert to B, where they would follow the same attack pattern, while simultaneously target C would be attacked by five Lancasters as a distraction from the attacks under way on targets A and B. After completing their attacks, individual crews were to make their own way home at low level and high speed.

During April and early May, test pilots 'Sam' Brown (Avro) and S/L M.V. Longbottom (on secondment from the RAF to Vickers), and Vickers' flight-test observer Bob Handasyde carried out a series of trial weapon drops in the sea off Reculver, between Herne Bay and Birchington. As a test area it offered better security than Chesil Beach in Dorset, and it also allowed easier recovery of the dropped weapons for examination. The first of several trials at this new test location took place on 13 April using a converted Wellington bomber and reduced size practice spheres. Two high-speed cine cameras were used to record the results and an observer marked on a Perspex screen the number of bounces made by each bomb. The first sphere to be dropped in this series of tests was released from a height of 250ft and broke up on hitting the sea; the second, although dropped from only 50ft, suffered some damage but succeeded in bouncing across the surface of the water for some distance. Three more spheres were test-dropped on 18 April, another on the 21st and one more on the 22nd. On 28 April further dropping trials were flown and from their results the final shape and size of the bouncing bomb was determined as a cylinder and not a sphere. Among the trial observers on this occasion were Barnes Wallis, accompanied by Guy Gibson.

On 1 May Longbottom dropped the first full-size Upkeep cylinder at Reculver. On the 11th, three of the new Type 464 Provisioning Lancasters of 617 Squadron for the first time dropped inert Upkeeps at Reculver, and the next day further aircraft from the squadron carried out more trial drops. Using dummy towers on the promenade as their targets, the Upkeep weapons bounced across the surface of the sea and bowled up the beach. These practice attacks continued for the next two days, but two precious aircraft were damaged in the process, one beyond repair. The tail plane of ED921, flown by Les Munro, was

Below: Watched by a small group of steely-nerved observers, including Gibson and Wallis, an inert Upkeep filled with concrete bounces off the sea and bowls up the beach at Reculver, at some time between 11 and 14 May 1943.
(IWM FLM2343)

damaged due to the practice Upkeep being dropped from below the prescribed 60ft, but happily the Lancaster was repairable in time for the operation itself. However, ED933, flown by Henry Maudslay, was badly damaged, and despite the best efforts of the workshop staff at Scampton, it was scrubbed from the battle order on the 16th. On the 13th, the only fully armed live Upkeep mine to be spun and dropped before the operation was released from a Lancaster in a trial 5 miles off the Kent coast at Broadstairs. A camera crew located at the North Foreland captured on film the resulting explosion, which raised a plume of water hundreds of feet into the air.

On the evening of the 14th, the nineteen specially modified Type 464 Provisioning Lancasters now available to the squadron flew their last exercise together before Operation Chastise. The following day, last-minute checks and adjustments were made to the weapon and its release mechanism after a second live Upkeep was dropped off Broadstairs, but this time without being spun.

The stage was now set for the big 'op', but as yet none of the crews knew the identity of their intended target. Speculation was rife, with the favourite being a low-level attack on the German battleship *Tirpitz*, but soon all would be revealed.

Opposite page, top and bottom: These superb head-on shots – once again movie stills – were probably taken on 11 May 1943 and capture the moment as Guy Gibson, having just released his Upkeep weapon over the Reculver range, pilots ED932, G for George, towards the camera and then thunders overhead with the Lancaster's four Merlins at full chat. Operation Chastise is less than a week away.
(IWM FLM2348/2353)

Above: On 13 May the only fully armed live Upkeep to be spun and dropped before Chastise was released from a Lancaster in a trial 5 miles off the Kent coast at Broadstairs.
(IWM FLM2365)

Above: W/C Guy Gibson enjoys a trick with his pet black labrador, Nigger. The popular dog was run over and killed by a car outside the camp gate at Scampton hours before Operation Chastise was due to begin.

(Bruce Robertson collection)

CHAPTER 4

OPERATION CHASTISE

'Operation Chastise. Immediate attack of targets X, Y and Z approved. Execute at first suitable opportunity.' With this top-secret message to HQ Bomber Command from the office of the Chief of the Air Staff on 15 May, the momentous decision to proceed with the attack on the Ruhr dams was taken. A staff car containing Cochrane was soon despatched from 5 Group HQ to drive the short distance to Scampton, where the AOC met with Whitworth and Gibson to inform them that the operation was on for the next day, 16 May. That evening, Gibson and Wallis briefed the two flight commanders, Dinghy Young and Henry Maudslay, as well as John Hopgood (Gibson's deputy leader for the attack on the Möhne) and Bob Hay (the bombing leader), on the operation that was scheduled for the following night. After the informal briefing, Whitworth broke the sad news to Gibson that his faithful black Labrador companion, Nigger, had been killed in a road accident outside the camp's main gate. Some feared this was a bad omen for the forthcoming operation.

In the early afternoon of 16 May, Scampton's tannoy system crackled into life. 'All crews of No. 617 Squadron to report to the briefing room immediately.' The great secret was finally shared when Gibson and Wallis revealed details of the targets to 617's aircrew at a first briefing for the squadron's pilots and navigators, bomb aimers and gunners. Meanwhile, 5 Group's chief signals officer, W/C Dunn, briefed the wireless operators on the special signals requirements for the night ahead. Crews also had the opportunity to study reconnaissance photographs of their targets as well as the carefully made scale models of the Möhne and Sorpe dams, built by the RAF Central Interpretation Unit's model section in Danesfield House at Medmenham, in the Thames Valley.

In the hangars and out on the dispersals the ground crews struggled to ensure that every aircraft was serviceable and ready for war. Petrol

bowsers pumped 10,800lbs of 100 octane fuel into each aircraft's six self-sealing tanks; teams of armourers toiled to feed the front and rear turrets with 18,000 and 12,000 rounds of tracer ammunition respectively. However, Lancaster ED933, which had been damaged by Maudslay during practice on 13 May, was declared beyond repair in time for the operation, leaving only nineteen of the modified Lancasters available. Sickness meant that the crews of P/O William Divall and F/L Harold Wilson who had been slated for the operation would not be flying after all. This was fortuitous, since there would have been insufficient aircraft available for them.

The weather had been unseasonably hot that day, and the air was still very warm when the final and formal briefing for all aircrew was held at 1800hrs in the upstairs briefing room at Scampton. When the platform party of Gibson, Wallis, G/C Whitworth and Air Vice-Marshal Cochrane swept in and made their way to the front of the briefing room, the crews quickly realised the significance of the operation they were soon to be called upon to fly. Gibson told the gathered crews to sit down, and drawing aside the blackout curtain that covered the large map of Germany on the wall, he boldly announced to the expectant audience that their target for that night was the great dams of western Germany. Wallis was then introduced and the softly spoken, white haired scientist ran through again what he had said on 15 May, and indeed earlier that day. He explained why the dams had been chosen for attack and outlined some of the problems he had encountered in developing the special weapon they would be using later that night. Once Wallis had finished his briefing, the AOC stood up and gave the crews a pep talk. He swore them to secrecy about the details of the weapon and finished with the remark, 'Now you are off on a raid that will do a tremendous amount of damage. It will become historic.' His words were prophetic.

When Cochrane stood down from the platform, Gibson rose to run through the operational details once again. The first wave comprising three sections of three aircraft consisted of Gibson, Hopgood, Martin, Young, Astell, Maltby, Maudslay, Knight and Shannon. They would take off at ten-minute intervals and fly the southern route from Scampton, across the North Sea to make landfall over the Scheldt estuary, between Noord Beveland and Schouwen, and thence to the Möhne dam (Target X), where they were to press home their attack until the dam had definitely been breached. Once the Möhne had been breached, the remaining aircraft of the first wave that were still carrying mines would divert to the Eder dam (Target Y), where the same procedure would be followed until that dam had also been breached. When the Möhne and the Eder had both been breached, those aircraft still with mines would fly on to the Sorpe dam (Target Z). In the meantime the second wave of five Lancasters, comprising McCarthy, Byers, Barlow, Rice and Munro, would take off singly and

Opposite: Guy Gibson in contemplative mood. At the time of Chastise he was a 24-year-old veteran pilot, having already completed 170 flying sorties as a bomber and night fighter pilot. He is pictured here wearing a non-regulation captured German Schwimmweste, the Luftwaffe equivalent of the RAF's Mae West. These gas-inflated life vests were highly prized among RAF aircrew.
(IWM CH11047)

Overleaf: Gibson with four of his crew, photographed after the dams raid. Fred Spafford (bomb aimer), Bob Hutchison (wireless operator), George Deering (front gunner), and Torger Taerum (navigator).
(IWM TR1127)

CODE WORDS FOR USE ON OPERATION CHASTISE

Pranger – Attack Target X (Möhne)
Nigger – Target X breached, divert to Target Y (Eder)
Dinghy – Target Y breached, divert to Target Z (Sorpe)
Danger – Attack target D (Lister)
Edward – Attack Target E (Ennepe)
Fraser – Attack Target F (Henne, later changed to Diemel)
Gilbert – Attack last resort targets as detailed
Goner – Special weapon released
Mason – All aircraft return to Base

ALPHA NUMERIC CODES FOR USE ON OPERATION CHASTISE

X – Möhne (changed to 'A' in signals order)
Y – Eder (changed to 'B' in signals order)
Z – Sorpe (changed to 'C' in signals order)
D – Lister
E – Ennepe
F – Diemel

Note: *The appropriate letter was to be added after the following number code. For example, 'Goner 68A' means that the Upkeep weapon had been released at the Möhne dam and it had exploded close to (5yds) the dam wall, but with no apparent effect.*

Goner 1 – Special weapon released, failed to explode
Goner 2 – Special weapon released, overshot dam
Goner 3 – Special weapon released, exploded more than 100yds from dam
Goner 4 – Special weapon released, exploded 100yds from dam
Goner 5 – Special weapon released, exploded 50yds from dam
Goner 6 – Special weapon released, exploded 5yds from dam
Goner 7 – Special weapon released, exploded in contact with dam
Goner 8 – No apparent breach
Goner 9 – Small breach in dam
Goner 10 – Large breach in dam

fly the northern route across the North Sea to the Dutch island of Vlieland before turning south-east over the Zuider Zee (Ijsselmeer) to join the same route as the first wave, at a point north-west of the German town of Wesel. The third wave, consisting of five aircraft, captained by Townsend, Anderson, Brown, Ottley and Burpee, considered as a 'mobile reserve', would take off two and a half hours later and fly the same southern route as the first wave. Its brief was to attack the 'last resort' targets of the Lister (Target D), Ennepe (Target E), and Diemel (Target F) dams.

Aircraft were to cross England at 1,500ft before descending to low level to cross the North Sea. At this point they were to set their altimeters to 60ft and maintain this low level all the way to the target. They were expected to fly at the same low level on the way home, at least until they had left the enemy coast behind. Low-level flying was vital to avoid the unwelcome attentions of German radar, flak and night fighters.

As a final summary of what was expected that night, Gibson outlined the routes to be followed to and from the targets, and confirmed timings, code words and other operational details for the three waves of aircraft. The briefing ended at 1930hrs and crews made their way to their respective messes for the traditional pre-op meal of bacon and eggs.

Below: With minutes to go before boarding G for George, Bob Hutchison exchanges a few words with Gibson, who is fastening his parachute harness.
(IWM CH9682)

Beneath a leaden sky, the steely-looking crew of F/L Joe McCarthy (AJ-T) sit for the photographer. From left to right, Sgt G.L. Johnson (bomb-aimer), P/O D.A. MacLean (navigator), Sgt R. Batson (front gunner), F/L Joe McCarthy (pilot), Sgt W.G. Radcliffe (engineer), and Sgt L. Eaton (wireless operator). Missing from this picture is F/O D. Rodger, the rear gunner.

(IWM TR1128)

Freezing a moment in time, this historic photograph captures Gibson and his crew as they hesitate briefly for the camera before climbing inside G for George on the evening of 16 May. Only four of the nine photographs taken before and after the raid were passed by the censor for publication, such was the security surrounding Chastise. From left to right: Trevor-Roper, Pulford, Deering, Spafford, Hutchison, Gibson and Taerum.
(IWM CH18005)

In the meantime, Bomber Command HQ had made contact with RAF Benson to inform them of the exact time of the attack, so that PR coverage of the results could be obtained as early as possible the next morning by putting an aircraft over the targets soon after first light.

An entry written in the squadron record book by F/L Harry Humphries, 617's adjutant, conveys something of the special mood in the air at Scampton in the hours before take-off:

This was Der Tag for 617 Squadron. Hardly a soul with the exception of the crews knew the target. Very few people outside the squadron knew we were operating – not even the WAAFs. From eight o'clock onwards the scenes outside the crew rooms were something to be remembered. It was not like an ordinary operational scene, all the crews on this occasion being aware of the terrific task confronting them. Most of them wore expressions varying from the 'don't care a damn' to the grim and determined. On the whole I think it appeared rather reminiscent of a crusade.

In the locker rooms the crews changed into their flying kit. Valuables were handed in for safekeeping and escape kits collected. Sandwiches and flasks of coffee for the return journey, together with slabs of Fry's Sandwich chocolate and barley sugar sweets, were handed out to each man from wrappings of newspaper. Outside the locker room the buses arrived to take the crews on the bumpy ride to their aircraft dispersed around the airfield. A corporal stood at the open door shouting out the letters by which each aircraft was known. As space became available on a bus for that aircraft's crew, they climbed on board and were driven out to their waiting Lancaster.

At 2110hrs Gibson's wireless operator, F/L Bob Hutchison, fired a red Very light into the cloudless evening sky, signalling that all aircraft in the first and second waves should start engines. Looking out of the cockpit window to the ground below, Gibson's flight engineer, Sgt John Pulford, called back to his skipper that the ground crew were ready to start the port inner. Switching on the ignition and booster coil, Pulford pressed the starter button on the cockpit instrument panel and the first of the four 1,480hp Rolls-Royce Merlin 28 engines coughed, spluttered and finally burst into life. The same procedure was repeated by fourteen aircraft until the air became alive with the sound of fifty-six Merlin engines being warmed up to operating temperature.

The Lancasters taxied in stately progress around the airfield perimeter track to the take-off point. Because they were flying the longer northerly route, the aircraft from the second wave were the first to take off. At 2128hrs Operation Chastise got under way as the first aircraft of the second wave, piloted by F/L Bob Barlow, lumbered off Scampton's grass runway, followed at one-minute intervals by the remaining four aircraft. However, a coolant leak in AJ-Q forced F/L Joe McCarthy to rapidly switch his crew to the reserve aircraft, AJ-T, but

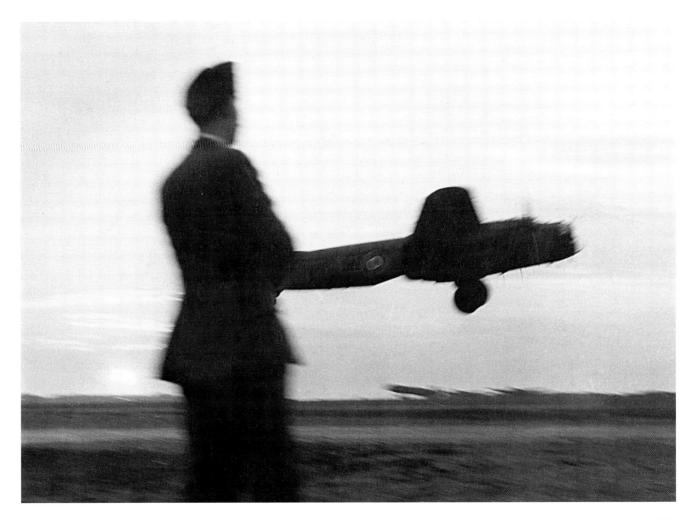

Above: Operation Chastise gets under way: an unidentified Lancaster of 617 Squadron takes off from Scampton's grass runway and climbs away into a cloudless dusk sky.
(IWM CH18006)

this too was unserviceable due to the absence of the compass deviation card. Without this, accurate flying along the carefully charted route to the dams would be impossible. Fortunately, the squadron's senior NCO, F/S G.E. 'Chiefy' Powell, had met the furious McCarthy on his way to the instrument section and had miraculously located the missing card. AJ-T was now ready for business and took off twenty minutes late, behind the rest of the second-wave aircraft that were already heading into the gathering dusk, eastwards across the North Sea.

At 2139hrs the green Aldis light winked through the twilight from the chequered flare-path caravan, giving take-off clearance to Gibson. The four Merlin engines of AJ-G were run up against the wheel brakes, and with a hiss of compressed air the brakes were released, the throttles were advanced and the Lancaster lurched forward on its take-off run. The aircraft of Hopgood (AJ-M) and Martin (AJ-P) joined G for George on either side. They were soon followed by Young (AJ-A), Maltby (AJ-J) and Shannon (AJ-L) at 2147hrs, and Maudslay (AJ-Z), Astell (AJ-B) and Knight (AJ-N) at 2159hrs.

The first wave was now airborne and Gibson led it by the fast fading light of the setting sun to the Wash and on towards the south-east, crossing out over the English coast at Southwold. Flying low across the North Sea to escape detection by German radar, strict radio silence was

Scampton

2nd wave

Lincoln

1st and 3rd wave

AJ-A

GREAT BRITAIN

London

Antwerp

0 miles 50

0 kilometres 60

FRANCE

BELGIUM

92

outward route
return route
outward turning point
return turning point
outward loss
return loss

AJ-H aborted here
AJ-W aborted here
AJ-K

GERMANY

HOLLAND

rdam

Munster

AJ-Z
AJ-E

AJ-S

AJ-B
AJ-C
AJ-M

Essen
Gladbeck
Dortmund
Möhne Dam (breached 0056hrs)
R.Ruhr
Hagen
Krefeld
Sorpe Dam
Kassel
Wuppertal
Mönchengladbach
R. Rhine
R. Eder
Ennepe Dam
Eder Dam
(breached 0150hrs)
Cologne

100
150

observed. With the first traces of moonlight dancing along a narrow silver pathway across the dark waters skimming by close beneath their wings, Gibson and the first wave made landfall on the Dutch coast. They were a few miles further south than planned, over the heavily defended island of Walcheren, but quickly corrected their course towards Roosendaal. Looking around him, Gibson noticed with satisfaction that Hopgood and Martin were still there and flying in perfect formation alongside him.

As luck would have it, they had taken the enemy defences by surprise and no flak rose to greet them. Gibson recalls in *Enemy Coast Ahead* that they were flying very low. 'We were flying so low that more than once Spam [Spafford] yelled at me to pull up quickly to avoid high-tension wires and tall trees.' At Roosendaal, a further course change saw them head almost due east to follow the glistening ribbon of the Wilhelmina Canal that took them between the Luftwaffe nightfighter bases at Gilze Rijen and Eindhoven. Some distance further on, at the town of Beek, the canal intersected with another waterway, the Zuid Willemsvaart, in a T-junction which was the landmark for the formation to turn towards the River Rhine and the German frontier. Realising they were off course again, in fact some 6 miles too far to the south, Gibson banked sharply to port and flew up the Rhine in the direction of Rees before turning east towards Ahsen and the cluster of small lakes at Dulmen.

Over the Rhine the formation received its first dose of enemy fire from flak gunners on river barges, whose rounds were eagerly returned by the Lancasters' vigilant gunners. In the Borken area a heavy concentration of flak and searchlights caused difficulties, while north-west of Dorsten proved to be another hot spot, with all three lead aircraft caught in the blinding glare of probing searchlights. Thundering across the German countryside at tree-top height, more trouble awaited as the first wave flew towards Dulmen, where light flak damaged the port wing of Hopgood's AJ-M. This caused Gibson to break radio silence and call up 5 Group headquarters with a flak warning for the aircraft that were following. Flying north of the notorious town of Hamm with its heavily defended railway marshalling yards, Gibson's first flight of three Lancasters approached its final major turning point at Ahlen, from where it flew due south in the velvet darkness between the sleeping towns of Werl and Soest towards the distant Ruhr hills. The first flight arrived over the Möhne dam at 0020hrs. 'As we came over the hill,' wrote Gibson, 'we saw the Möhne Lake. Then we saw the dam itself. In that light it looked squat and heavy and unconquerable.'

Some 6 minutes behind Gibson was the second flight of three Lancasters led by S/L Dinghy Young in AJ-A, with Maltby (AJ-J) and Shannon (AJ-L), who reached the Möhne at 0026hrs. They too had encountered flak en route, but it was the third flight of the first wave led by S/L Henry Maudslay in AJ-Z that suffered the first fatality of the night. Shortly after crossing into Germany from Holland, Astell's Lancaster (AJ-B) was flying at the prescribed low level, but appeared to hesitate at a course change. Astell failed to turn with Maudslay and Knight, and lagged behind. Near the village of Marbeck, AJ-B flew into an electricity pylon, whereupon the aircraft erupted into a ball of flame and staggered on a little further before crashing in a field. Several minutes later the mine exploded with devastating consequences. All seven crew died.

To give the attacking aircraft as much protection as possible from defensive flak on and around the dam wall itself, the Lancasters were to dive over the Körbecke road bridge that spanned the Möhne lake. Each aircraft would then fly along the lake before turning and climbing a little to cross over the wooded Hever promontory, then dropping down to the prescribed attack height again on the final one-mile run-in to the dam. This still left the aircraft to adjust their height and speed on the most crucial phase of their bombing run, vulnerable to the withering gunfire from enemy flak positions.

Gibson flew over the Möhne dam in a dummy run to investigate the defences, braving the concentrated fire of some twelve light flak guns situated on the sluice towers, dam wall and in the fields that surrounded the dam. He recalls: 'It was light flak, mostly green, yellow and red, and the colours of the tracer reflected upon the face of the water in the lake. The reflections on the dead calm of the black water made it seem there was twice as much as there really was.' Pleased with what he had observed and unscathed by the attentions of the German gunners, Gibson called up the five other aircraft and prepared them to commence their individual attack runs on his command. 'Hello, all Cooler aircraft. I am going to attack. Stand by to come in to attack in your order when I tell you.'

CHAPTER 5

BREACHING
THE DAMS

The moment of truth had arrived. It marked the culmination of months of intensive training by Gibson and his crews, not to mention years of toil and trial by Barnes Wallis, who had invented the bouncing bomb. As Gibson began his attack he called up Hopgood, his deputy in AJ-M: 'Hello, "M Mother". Stand by to take over if anything happens.'

Skimming over the tree-tops of the Hever promontory, P/O Torger Taerum, the navigator, switched on the twin Aldis lamps and talked Gibson down to the attack height as he banked AJ-G onto the final leg

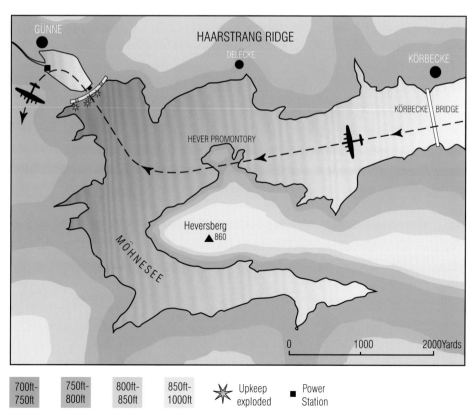

Left: Map of the Möhne dam and its environs, showing the local topography and the direction of attack.

(Bow Watkinson)

towards the target. The Lancaster was now established at a height of
60ft and a speed of 230mph, but Gibson sweated at the controls of the
heavy bomber to keep her dead on track towards the great dam wall
that loomed menacingly ahead in the clear light of the moon.
A ferocious curtain of twinkling flak was hurled towards them.
Appearing lazy at first, its glowing tracers seemed to suddenly
accelerate as they hissed past.

F/L Bob Hutchison, the wireless operator, checked the rotation speed
of the Upkeep mine at 500rpm while down in the bomb aimer's
compartment in the nose, P/O Fred Spafford watched the glistening
black waters of the lake rush by beneath him as he lined up the twin
towers in his Dann sight. Immediately above Spafford in the front
turret, F/S Joe Deering opened up with everything he had, hosing the
towers of the dam with tracer from his twin .303in Brownings.

Gibson's description of the final moments leading to his attack are
memorable: 'Spam said "Left – little more left – steady – steady –
steady – coming up." Of the next few seconds I remember only a series
of kaleidoscopic incidents. The chatter from Joe's front guns pushing
out tracers which bounced off the left-hand flak tower. Pulford
crouching beside me. The smell of burnt cordite. The cold sweat
underneath my oxygen mask. The tracers flashing past the windows –
they all seemed the same colour now – and the inaccuracy of the gun
positions near the power station; they were firing in the wrong
direction. The closeness of the dam wall. Spam's exultant, "Mine
gone." Hutch's red Very lights to blind the flak gunners. The speed of
the whole thing.'

AJ-G thundered over the dam wall and from his vantage point in the
rear turret, F/L Dick Trevor-Roper could see their weapon bouncing
across the lake to hit the dam. As they circled round in the moonlit sky,
Gibson's crew witnessed the terrific explosion as their mine detonated,
throwing a huge column of seething white water hundreds of feet into
the air. They seemed certain that with such a blast the dam could not
possibly hold. 'The surface of the lake and the water had become
broken and furious,' recalled Gibson, 'as though it were being lashed
by a gale. At first we thought that the dam itself had broken because
great sheets of water were slopping over the top of the wall like a
gigantic basin.' But once the waters of the lake had subsided it became
evident that the dam had held. Hutchison signalled 5 Group HQ
'Goner 68A', which indicated that their mine had exploded but without
breaching the dam.

Gibson called up Hopgood to attack, and M for Mother began its
run-in over the trees of the Hever promontory towards the dam. The
twin Aldis spotlights could be clearly seen by Gibson's crew as
Hopgood's Lancaster descended over the lake to the bombing height of
60ft. But the enemy flak gunners had now got an idea from which
direction the attack was coming and they opened up with everything

they had, pouring deadly ribbons of tracer into M for Mother. When still about 300ft away from the dam wall Hopgood's Lancaster was hit in two engines and set on fire, and soon a tongue of vivid orange flame trailed from a ruptured fuel tank. In all the pandemonium Hopgood's bomb aimer, P/O Jim Fraser, released his Upkeep mine too late and instead of hitting the wall of the dam it bounced over the parapet, landing on the power station below that housed seven electrical transformers. There it exploded with a blinding flash. M for Mother staggered on for a short distance, Hopgood wrestling with the controls, desperately trying to gain height so that his crew could bale out, but the Lancaster was seen to explode in mid-air. One wing fell off and the wreckage tumbled into a meadow near the village of Ostonnen some three miles beyond the dam, where it burnt fiercely. Miraculously, P/Os Jim Fraser and Tony Burcher baled out and survived to become prisoners of war, but Sgt John Minchin was unlucky when his parachute failed to open fully and he fell to his death.

Gibson called Martin into the attack at 0038hrs. To draw some of the enemy fire off P for Popsy, Gibson flew slightly ahead of Martin before turning G for George over the dam to engage flak positions beyond the wall. Despite his aircraft receiving some hits, bomb aimer F/L Bob Hay released his Upkeep weapon. Moments later a huge explosion shook the waters of the lake once again and a plume of white spray was hurled hundreds of feet skywards. And once more, when the waters had subsided, the dam had still not been breached. F/O Chambers transmitted 'Goner 58A' to 5 Group HQ, informing them of another failure.

Next in line for the attack was Dinghy Young in AJ-A, who was accompanied on his run-in to the target by Martin in AJ-P, in a further attempt to draw some of the enemy flak. Gibson flew beyond the dam wall for his gunners to engage the enemy flak positions from the other side, switching on his aircraft identification lights to distract them from the approach of Young's Lancaster. AJ-A's Upkeep was released and hit the dam wall as intended. A huge explosion ensued, followed by a towering column of white water – but the dam held. 'Goner 78A' was transmitted to 5 Group HQ telling them of a further failure.

When at last the water had subsided, Gibson called up number five, David Maltby in AJ-J. This time, Gibson and Martin engaged enemy flak positions from the lake side of the dam as Maltby made his approach. From the cockpit of J for Jig he could make out that the dam structure had indeed been damaged by Young's Upkeep and that the crown of the wall was already crumbling. At 0049hrs Maltby released his mine, which bounced four times across the glassy black water before it struck the dam wall and exploded, throwing a glistening white water spout 1,000ft into the night sky. For some unexplained reason, Maltby's wireless operator, Sgt Stone, sent another 'Goner 78A' message to HQ at Grantham before waiting to observe the result of

Overleaf: Gibson and Martin use their Lancasters to draw enemy fire away from 'Dinghy' Young in AJ-A as he releases his Upkeep weapon over the Möhne lake. It took five Upkeeps to breach the wall of the Möhne, with Maltby's weapon finally cracking open the structure at 0056hrs.

(From an original painting by Nicolas Trudgian, courtesy of The Military Gallery, Bath)

99

their attack. Gibson, realising that time was getting short, called up Dave Shannon in AJ-L and told him to prepare to attack. As he turned in to make his bombing run, Gibson noticed to his amazement that water was beginning to pour through the shattered dam wall.

'I heard someone shout, "I think she has gone! I think she has gone!" Other voices took up the cry and quickly I said, "Stand by until I make a recco."' Gibson ordered Shannon to abort his attack and turn away from the target, before flying towards the dam himself to take a closer look.

'Now there was no doubt about it; there was a great breach 100yds across, and the water, looking like stirred porridge in the moonlight, was gushing out and rolling into the Ruhr Valley . . .'. At 0056hrs, Gibson ordered Hutchison to tap out the signal 'Nigger' (the code word for success) to Grantham, who in turn repeated the message back to Hutchison for confirmation. The seven Lancasters that had survived so far came down from the hills around the lake, where they had been standing off, to have a closer look and see what had been done. Most of the flak had stopped by now, except for a lone gunner on the dam itself, but he was quickly silenced by a well-aimed burst of '303 from one of the Lancasters' gunners.

Writing in *Enemy Coast Ahead*, Gibson recalls: 'Now it was all quiet, except for the roar of the water which steamed and hissed its way from its 150-foot head. Then we began to shout and scream like madmen over the R/T, for this was a tremendous sight, a sight which probably no man will ever see again.'

Conscious of the fact that they had other dams to attack, Gibson silenced the R/T chatter and then called up all aircraft, telling Martin and Maltby to head for home and the rest (Shannon, Maudslay and Knight, with Young as deputy leader) to follow him to the Eder dam, 50 miles and 14 minutes' flying time to the south-east of the Möhne. They set course from the southern tip of the Möhne lake, which was already fast emptying itself of 176 million cubic yards of water. After some tricky low flying along the winding valleys that led to the Eder lake, the five aircraft finally reached their second target. It was not easy to pinpoint the dam itself because fog was already forming in the valleys, making it difficult to distinguish one part of the reservoir filled with water from another valley filled with fog.

Circling to allow Maudslay, Shannon and Astell to catch up, Gibson called up on the R/T to ask if they could see the target. Dave Shannon answered faintly that he thought he was nearby but couldn't find the dam. To aid him in identifying the Eder, Gibson fired a red Very light over the top of the dam, and within a few minutes all five Lancasters had rendezvoused and were flying a left-hand orbit over the target.

Situated in a deep valley surrounded by high hills densely clad with pine forest, the Eder dam was much more inaccessible and altogether a more difficult target than the Möhne. North of the dam lay the

Opposite: Mission accomplished: the breached Möhne dam, photographed by a high-flying Spitfire PRXI from RAF Benson on the morning after the raid. Brown mud banks fringe the reservoir and the contents of the Möhne lake are rapidly emptying through a massive breach measuring over 300ft across.

(IWM CH9687)

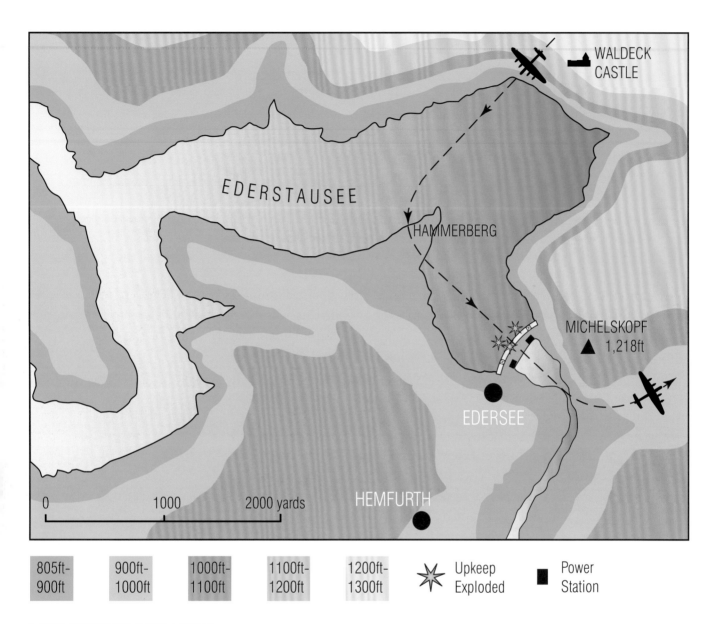

EDERSTAUSEE

WALDECK CASTLE

HAMMERBERG

MICHELSKOPF
▲ 1,218ft

EDERSEE

HEMFURTH

| 0 | 1000 | 2000 yards |

| 805ft-900ft | 900ft-1000ft | 1000ft-1100ft | 1100ft-1200ft | 1200ft-1300ft | ✳ Upkeep Exploded | ▪ Power Station |

Above: Map of the Eder dam and its environs, showing the local topography and the direction of attack.

(Bow Watkinson)

Opposite: A pilot's-eye view from Waldeck castle, looking down onto the Ederstausee, with the Hammerberg spit in the middle foreground, and beyond (half-hidden by the forested promontory on the left) is the Eder dam itself. Behind the dam is the Michelskopf, the high ground that the attacking aircraft needed to climb and bank hard to avoid after releasing their mines. From this photograph, it can be appreciated how the topography around the Eder lake made it extremely difficult to fly an accurate approach to the dam.

(Richard Simms)

impressive medieval Waldeck castle with its commanding views across the Eder lake. To make a successful approach to the dam itself, the Lancasters would need to dive steeply over the castle from 1,000ft, then fly along the shallow gorge that led onto the lake, before encountering the wooded Hammerberg spit which forms a natural barrier in front of the dam itself. A tight turn to port would then be made over the spit, followed by a drop down to the attack height of 60ft for the run-in to the target, now less than a mile distant. If the flying was demanding, there was one consolation in that the dam had no flak defences.

Conscious of time ticking away and dawn drawing ever nearer, Gibson ordered Shannon to commence his attack. He circled wide and then turned L for Love to go in. Diving down rather too steeply, sparks came from his engines as he had to pull out at full boost to avoid hitting the hillside. He tried three or more times without releasing his mine, unable to establish himself at the correct height for the attack after executing the steep dive followed by the sharp turn over the

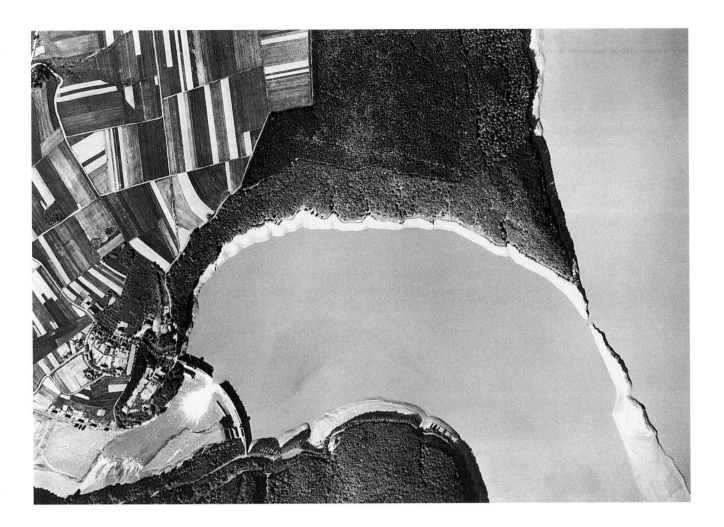

Above: Further reconnaissance photographs painted a similar picture of destruction at the Eder dam, where it took three Upkeeps to break open the dam wall.

(IWM CH9750)

Hammerberg spit. He stepped aside to allow Maudslay to commence his attack, but he too found it difficult to achieve the correct height and speed in two abortive attempts. Shannon returned to the fray and made two dummy runs before finally releasing his mine at 0139hrs. The weapon was seen to strike the dam wall and explode, followed by a towering column of white water that reached almost 1,000ft into the sky. Maudslay then began his third run up to the dam and dropped his mine, but it was released too late. The weapon struck the dam parapet and exploded on contact with a 'slow, yellow, vivid flame which lit up the whole valley like daylight for just a few seconds'. Maudslay had flown on over the dam and appeared to be in trouble now as his Lancaster was seen banking steeply before disappearing from view. At the time it was assumed that he had crashed after being caught in the blast from his Upkeep mine, but it was later discovered that he had crossed the dam before the mine had exploded and was on his way home when he fell victim to flak at Emmerich/Klein-Netterden at 0236hrs.

The Eder dam was still unbroken so Gibson called up Astell at 0147hrs, but received no reply. Unknown to Gibson, Astell and his crew were dead, their Lancaster having crashed just inside the German border 97 minutes earlier. Now, only Knight in AJ-N was available to breach the Eder, and Gibson ordered him in to attack. With the last Upkeep left to do the job, he too encountered the same difficulties that Shannon and Maudslay had done earlier, but on his second run Mother Luck was on his side. Gibson recalls how 'we were flying above him, and about 400 yards to the right, and saw his mine hit the water. We saw where it sank. We saw the tremendous earthquake which shook the base of the dam, and then, as if a gigantic hand had punched a hole through cardboard, the whole thing collapsed.' Knight and his engineer, Sgt Ray Grayston, required all their strength to haul AJ-N up and out from behind the dam to clear the high ground of the Michelskopf that loomed ahead.

At 0154hrs, Hutchison sent the triumphant signal 'Dinghy' to 5 Group HQ, telling them the good news of the demise of the Eder dam. By now, Shannon and Knight had already turned for home and they set course for the Möhne lake to see for themselves how it had been emptying. Base signalled Hutchison, asking if they had any more aircraft in their wave available to attack the third target. The answer was 'No, none'.

At the Sorpe dam, 6 miles south-west of the Möhne, Joe McCarthy (of the second wave) and Ken Brown (third wave) had already completed their attacks, after making twelve dummy runs each before dropping their mines. The second wave of Lancasters had taken off before Gibson and had flown the northerly route across the North Sea to the Sorpe. To confuse the enemy defences and keep them guessing as to the real intentions of the bombers, they made their landfall some 125 miles to the north, but over the Dutch island of Texel the second wave suffered its first casualty. Light flak was responsible for damage inflicted on F/L Les Munro's Lancaster (AJ-W), which lost both its VHF radio and its intercom as a result, forcing him to abort his sortie and return to Scampton, where he landed at 0030hrs, the Upkeep still clasped beneath the belly of W for William.

Crossing the Dutch coast, P/O Vernon Byers in AJ-K was shot down by a 105mm flak gun, his aircraft crashing into the sea in flames off the southern tip of Texel. Meanwhile, F/O Geoff Rice in Lancaster AJ-H was flying so low that his aircraft grazed the surface of the sea near the island of Vlieland, the impact ripping off the Upkeep mine and tearing a gaping hole in the Lancaster's belly. With the fuselage awash with sea water, he was forced to abort the sortie and nurse his badly damaged aircraft back to Scampton, where he landed at 0050hrs, lucky to have made it home.

The perilous nature of low flying in a heavy bomber aircraft at night claimed the lives of F/L Bob Barlow and his crew in Lancaster AJ-E. They struck the top of an electricity pylon along the River Rhine near Rees and the aircraft crashed in flames at Haldern-Herken. Their Upkeep did not explode on impact and the self-destruction charge

Overleaf: The Sorpe defied the combined efforts of F/L Joe McCarthy (AJ-T) and Sgt Ken Brown (AJ-F) to make a breach in its concrete and earth wall. Two mines were dropped and the parapet damaged for a length of about 200ft, but the dam remained largely unscathed.

(Crown Copyright)

SORPE DAM
(After attack)
K 1559
Neg. No. 24689

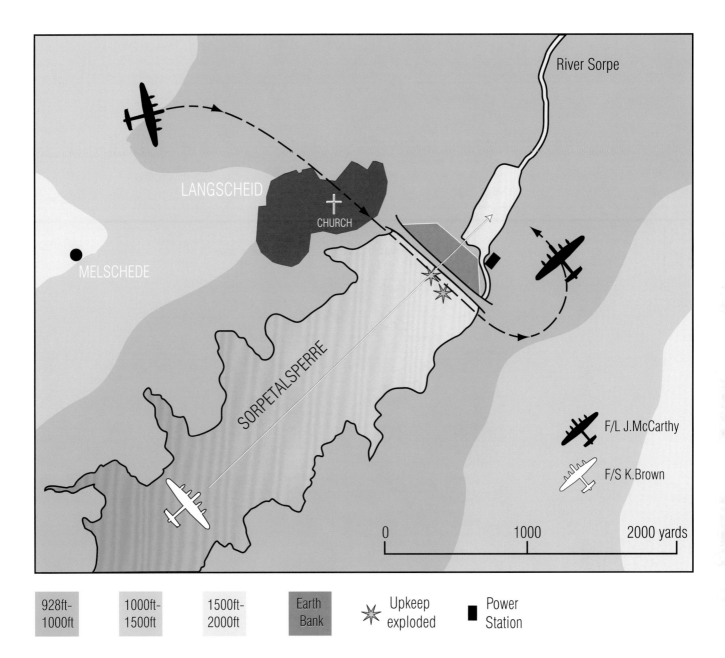

River Sorpe

LANGSCHEID

CHURCH

MELSCHEDE

SORPETALSPERRE

F/L J.McCarthy

F/S K.Brown

0   1000   2000 yards

| 928ft-1000ft | 1000ft-1500ft | 1500ft-2000ft | Earth Bank | ✳ Upkeep exploded | ■ Power Station |

failed to go off. The mine was successfully defused by a German bomb disposal team and eventually contributed a great deal to the Nazis' knowledge of the bouncing bomb.

Having taken off 34 minutes late due to a string of technical problems, McCarthy flew at 200mph, and had made up some of the lost time when he crossed the Dutch coast at Vlieland at 2331hrs. By now the German flak gunners were wide awake and looking for trouble, but flying at tree-top height McCarthy skilfully avoided major incident, although AJ-T collected a bullet in the starboard undercarriage nacelle. Four of the five aircraft in the second wave had either been forced to abort or had crashed, leaving only McCarthy to continue to the Sorpe, where he arrived at about 0015hrs. He encountered the same problem that Gibson and the others had found at the Eder, with thick mist in the valleys causing difficulty in pinpointing

Above: Map of the Sorpe dam and its environs, showing the local topography and the direction of attack.

(Bow Watkinson)

Lying broken on a beach in Holland, the wreckage of a Lancaster bears silent witness to the losses sustained by 617 Squadron on the dams raid. This aircraft is possibly ED877/AJ-A, flown by S/L Henry 'Dinghy' Young, shot down crossing the Dutch coast north of Ijmuiden on its homeward journey from bombing the Möhne dam.

(Crown Copyright)

NICOLAS TRUDGIAN © 2000.

Previous page: Homeward bound: after bombing the Eder dam, F/L David Shannon in Lancaster AJ-L races the dawn for home, at low level across the flat landscape of Holland.

(From an original painting by Nicolas Trudgian, courtesy of The Military Gallery, Bath)

the dam. When at last the dam was identified it was lit by bright moonlight from a cloudless sky, and McCarthy began his bombing run that led him over the sleeping village of Langscheid and along the crest of the 2,297ft-long dam wall. The reserve aircraft in which he was flying had not been fitted with the twin Aldis spotlights that were necessary for accurate height keeping, and so it took nine attempts before McCarthy's bomb aimer, Sgt George Johnson, was satisfied with AJ-T's height and line of flight. At 0046hrs, on the tenth run, Johnson released his Upkeep mine close to the centre of the dam wall, without any rotation and from a height of about 30ft. The resulting explosion sent a huge shower of water high into the sky, but when McCarthy flew back across the dam to inspect the result of his attack it became clear that the dam wall itself had survived, with only the parapet suffering damage.

Turning his Lancaster about and setting a course for home, McCarthy soon overflew what was left of the Möhne dam and its fast-emptying lake, but before long AJ-T became lost. In time the crew found themselves flying over the heavily defended railway marshalling yards at Hamm, at the perilously low height of 50ft – and certainly not the place for a heavy bomber to linger. Fortunately luck was on their side and they managed to escape without damage by heading towards the cluster of lakes near Dulmen. Still uncertain of their position, McCarthy finally opted to retrace the track of their outward-bound route instead of following the official track agreed at the briefing. AJ-T landed back on Scampton's turf at 0323hrs, but the flak hit they had taken on the outward flight had punctured a main wheel tyre, and so the touchdown was a little bumpy.

F/S Ken Brown had taken off at 0012hrs, the third aircraft in the reserve wave, and crossed the enemy coast at 0130hrs. Flying at low level over the hostile landscape of occupied Europe, AJ-F received the unwelcome attention of light flak. On several occasions Brown was forced to take violent evasive action when electricity pylons and tall trees loomed out of the darkness ahead of his aircraft. Nearing the target area, AJ-F's wireless operator received word from 5 Group HQ that the Möhne dam had been breached and ordering them to the Sorpe. Poor visibility owing to fog in the valleys caused problems in identifying the dam, but as luck would have it the visibility improved in its immediate vicinity and Brown was able to carry out his first attack run. But, as with McCarthy before him, the Sorpe proved a difficult nut to crack and it took nine attempts before Brown's Upkeep mine was finally dropped at 0314hrs. Unlike McCarthy, Brown took a head-on approach to the dam across the lake and dropped his mine against the wall, but again without any spin on the weapon. In due course, the tower of water that followed the explosion fell away to reveal to eager eyes in the circling Lancaster that the dam wall was still intact. However, further damage had been done to the parapet of the dam and its stone crest had begun to crumble. The signal, 'Goner 78C', was transmitted to Grantham by Brown's wireless operator at 0323hrs: their mine had exploded against the dam wall but had not breached it.

Brown and his crew beat a path for home. Flying over the spectacular silver ribbon of floods that by now had engulfed the hapless valley below the Möhne dam, they flew on, falling foul of accurate predicted flak and blinding searchlights at Hamm, and later when crossing the Zuider Zee. At such low level, the glare of the searchlights that suffused the cockpit of AJ-F could have blinded Brown, but he crouched as low in the cockpit as he dared while still flying the aircraft. By dint of some masterly low flying and a strong helping of good luck, AJ-F escaped disaster to cross the North Sea in the early morning light and land safely at Scampton at 0533hrs.

Having fallen behind schedule since becoming the last Lancaster to take off, AJ-Y captained by F/S Cyril Anderson became lost. En route he had been ordered to attack the Diemel dam, but at 0228 hrs his target was changed to the Sorpe. With his rear turret unserviceable and the dawn creeping ever closer, he decided to turn back. He arrived home at Scampton at 0530hrs with his mine still onboard.

The last aircraft to attempt an attack on a Ruhr dam during Operation Chastise was AJ-O captained by P/O Bill Townsend. Having

Above: When F/L Bob Barlow's Lancaster (AJ-E) collided with an electricity pylon and crashed at Haldern-Herken, its Upkeep rolled clear of the wreckage and miraculously failed to go off. The mine was later recovered and defused by German bomb disposal experts, who succeeded in discovering many of its secrets.
(Via Alfred Price)

Bombenträger

Laufscheibe trägt Bombe

Auswuchtplatten
(Größe nach Bedarf)

Buchsen für Wasserdruckzünder MK XIV

Buchse für Abreißzünder (Zeitzünder)

75
75

120

verschweißt u. über
Schalzschicht

1370'

700'

510'

190'

27

12,5

10

90'

1235'

Dichtungsring (Klingerit)

Brit. Rotationswasserbombe 3900 kg

RA2/1832

X17

strich dunkelrot
Rostschutzfarbe)
Aufschrift weiß

Aufgegossene Schutzschicht aus Tri

50

13°

Sprengstoff: 42 % Tri
40 % Hexogen
18 % Aluminium
etwa 2600 kg

25°

Übertragungsladung
Tetryl 1820 gr.

Stahlscheibe

Dichtungs-
scheibe

Übertragungsladungen
Tetryl 1253 gr.

Rille für Riemen
zum Antriebsmotor

Antriebsscheibe wird bei
Abwurf weggeklappt

Schutzschicht aus Vergußmasse

6 Durchgehende Stehbolzen verhindern Herausspringen
der Stirndeckel beim Aufslag

Previous page: Just how thoroughly the mine was examined can be appreciated from these scale drawings of the 'British Spinning Water Bomb' produced by the Germans.

taken off from Scampton at 0014hrs, AJ-O made landfall over the enemy coast at 0131hrs and suffered the unwelcome attentions of light flak along much of its flight path as it thundered across Germany at tree-top height. At 0222hrs, Grantham signalled AJ-O to attack the Ennepe dam, the Möhne and Eder having been breached by this point. Routeing via the Möhne dam, it was with some difficulty that Townsend eventually found the Ennepe, thanks to rising mist in the surrounding valleys. Circling over the lake, it quickly became apparent to him and his bomb aimer, Sgt C.E. Franklin, that the approach to the dam was going to be very difficult due to a number of topographical factors. In the end it took them until their fourth attempt before Franklin was happy with the height, speed and line of their approach, to release his mine at 0337hrs. Climbing up and over the tree-clad hills behind the dam, Townsend banked AJ-O around and turned back for a low pass over the dam to inspect the damage made by his mine. The characteristic explosion of their mine had been followed by a towering waterspout, but the weapon had sunk far short of the wall and failed to breach the dam. At 0411hrs AJ-O's wireless operator, F/S George Chalmers, sent 'Goner 58E' to HQ at Grantham.

Like Brown, Townsend flew back over the fast-emptying Möhne dam before setting a course for home, a journey that was anything but an enjoyable experience. Pushing the control column forward and taking AJ-O down among the weeds to fly her as fast as he dared, Townsend needed his full concentration to avoid high-tension cables and towering trees that loomed ahead in their path. They crossed over the enemy coast after attracting the unwelcome attention of enemy flak and searchlights and made it safely back to Scampton, where AJ-O landed at 0615hrs, the final aircraft to arrive home from Operation Chastise.

A little over one hour after Townsend had throttled back AJ-O's over-stressed Merlins, switched off and climbed exhausted from the aircraft with his crew onto Scampton's sweet-smelling grass, a solitary PR Spitfire took off from RAF Benson and headed into the morning sun for the Ruhr dams more than 300 miles distant.

CHAPTER 6

THE AFTERMATH – GERMANY

In the Ruhr and Eder valleys a disaster of biblical proportions had been unleashed. The force of the floodwaters as they bore down the valleys from the breaches in the Möhne and Eder dams was so great that the waters swept away almost everything in their deafening path. People's homes were dashed to pieces like so much matchwood, railway bridges torn down, trees uprooted, people and livestock carried away in the unrelenting torrent. Some observers reported seeing trees stripped of their bark, with railway lines wrapped around them like giant corkscrews.

Left: Torrents of water were still rushing through the breach in the Möhne dam twelve hours after the raid.

(IWM HU4594)

Back in England, 542 Squadron had been warned of the time of the attack and that photo-reconnaissance would be required to monitor the result. The crews were up early to study the weather conditions, which appeared to be favourable. At 0730hrs on the morning of the 17th, a lone Spitfire PRXI piloted by F/O Jerry Fray took off from RAF Benson and climbed out over the North Sea, heading for Germany and the Ruhr dams. Its mission was to arrive over the target at the first photographic light and photograph the results of the raids.

Several hundred miles ahead of Fray and his Spitfire, flooding along the Ruhr Valley below the Möhne dam now extended for about 40 miles. The town of Neheim, which lay several miles downstream from the dam itself, had been cut clean in two by the floodwaters. At the valley's narrowest point between Niederense and Neheim, the water had achieved speeds of up to 18ft/sec and it had reportedly reached a level of more than 45 feet.

As luck would have it, visibility was good and this promised Fray some clear photographs to take back to Benson. At a distance of about 150 miles from the Möhne dam, Fray could see the chemical haze that hung over the German industrial heartland of the Ruhr, and, turning his head slightly, away to the east he noticed what he took to be a bank of cloud. As he flew closer it became apparent that this cloud was in fact the effect of the sun glinting on the floodwaters that had been unleashed from the dams some 30,000ft beneath him. Soon the sheer enormity of the inundation that had hit the Ruhr Valley became clear, and as he neared the Möhne dam he estimated that the floodwaters were about a mile wide. Eight hours after the attack, water was still gushing through the breach in the dam wall at a rate of between 53,000 and 70,000 cubic ft/sec, and the level of the water in the reservoir had fallen dramatically, leaving exposed brown mud flats around the edges. The upper reaches of the lake were completely dry, except for the small portion where the sluice gates had been closed. He carried out his photographic run over the Möhne before flying on to the Eder dam.

As Fray looked down from his Spitfire cockpit onto the virtually empty reservoir 6 miles beneath him, he observed that the damage in the Eder Valley was far greater. This was due largely to the fact that the breach in the dam was wider than that at the Möhne, allowing more than three-quarters of the contents of the reservoir to escape. In reality, the lake would have been almost impossible to pinpoint had it not been for the tell-tale white stain of water still pouring from the breach in the dam wall. Two days after the attack, water was still gushing through the breach. Fray made a second run over the Eder to take further photographs, but seeing two unidentified aircraft approaching from the north-east he decided to cut short his sortie and beat it home.

Writing not long afterwards in the RAF's secret *Coastal Command Quarterly Review* (the RAF's PR squadrons were under the operational control of Coastal Command), Fray recalls his homecoming to Benson:

Opposite: The sheer scale of the catastrophe at the Möhne dam can be appreciated from this dramatic photograph. In the foreground lies a tangle of anti-torpedo netting and floats, washed through the breach by the relentless floodwaters. (*Bundesarchiv 1011/637/4192/27*)

While I was landing, I could see scrambled egg at the end of the runway. It was the station commander and I wondered if I had done anything wrong. But he was only waiting to welcome me home. When I landed he came up to me and said, 'Have they hit them?' and I was able to answer, 'Yes, they've pranged two of them properly. The floods are spreading for miles.' So he went off to telephone the news to Bomber Command.

At Benson the atmosphere was electric as the films were rushed from Fray's Spitfire and immediately developed. The first negatives to be processed from the damage assessment sortie were taken out of the drying cabinet and placed on the light table for examination. Everyone was there, from the station commander down, and they all crowded around F/L Ronald Gillanders, who was in charge of the day shift of damage interpreters at Medmenham. He had been ordered over to Benson by the Air Ministry so as to be there when Fray landed. As soon as the negatives were ready for viewing, he was to telephone G/C McNeil, Assistant Director of Photographic Intelligence at the Air Ministry, with the results of the initial interpretation.

The first frames of negatives showed nothing but floodwater – acres of it. Then Gillanders came to the Möhne dam and with the pin-sharp negative before him, he phoned McNeil – there was a gap

123

Debris litters the floor of the compensating basin in the shadow of the Möhne dam.

(Bundesarchiv 1011/637/4192/23)

Above: A photographic mosaic of the Möhne lake and its hinterland. The sheer size of the lake can be appreciated when compared to the dam itself, seen at top left.

(Bruce Robertson collection)

right in the centre of the dam, about 200ft across, and water was pouring through it.

Speaking afterwards, Gillanders admitted to being a little worried:

For a minute I did not recognise the place. I feared for a moment that they had bombed the wrong dam. I looked for the power station, but it had gone. The place which I had studied in great detail for many months looked completely different, and it was only on a second look that I recognised the familiar landmarks and realised that the reservoir was practically empty.

Once all the photographs had been printed and interpreted it became very clear that the Möhne and Eder dams had been breached, but that the Sorpe was damaged and still intact. Benson despatched a further PR sortie at 1045hrs and a third one in the same afternoon to add to the first coverage obtained by Fray.

Overleaf: The Möhne lake, largely drained of water, is pictured at the point where the road bridge crosses south of Delecke. *(IWM CH9721)*

Above: The floods swept away factory buildings in Neheim – the foundations in the foreground are all that remain.

(RAF Museum PC71/19/356/43)

Opposite: The Ruhr Valley at Frondenberg, 13 miles downstream from the Möhne dam. It was at this point that the floodwaters spread out across the full width of the valley. At 'A' stood a hutted camp for Russian PoWs, washed away by the inundation; at 'B' the road and rail bridges that linked Frondenberg to Menden were also swept away (and see overleaf).

(Crown Copyright)

Photo-reconnaissance confirmed that material damage in both the Ruhr and Eder valleys was extensive, but was far more serious along the Möhne and Ruhr valleys, where the river beds were badly silted up below Neheim. In places the rivers had altered their course and in time it would be necessary to divert them back along their old beds. Large gravel banks had also formed and effectively cut off the valley, hindering drainage of the floodwaters. In the shadow of the Möhne dam wall, the power station had been completely destroyed, along with the compensating basin, while the smaller power station situated a little further south was so heavily damaged as to be beyond repair. Further downstream, heavy damage had been caused to many more waterworks and power stations, mainly through the action of mud, silt and the undermining of the structures.

Writing after the war in his memoirs, *Inside the Third Reich*, Hitler's Armaments Minister Albert Speer recalled:

The report that reached me in the early hours of the morning was most alarming. The largest of the dams, the Mohne dam, had been shattered and the reservoir emptied. As yet there were no reports on the three other dams. At dawn we landed at Werl airfield, having first surveyed the scene of devastation

All that remained of the double-track steel railway bridge at Fröndenberg that was ripped from its piers and carried more than 330ft downstream by the floodwaters. The toppled steelwork of the bridge can be seen in the top left of the photograph, with the masonry piers towards the centre.

(Bundesarchiv 1011/637/4194/5A)

Right: Some 18ft up from the ground, bark was stripped from tree trunks by the ferocity of the floodwaters.

(RAF Museum PC71/19/356/17)

from above. The power plant at the foot of the shattered dam looked as if it had been erased, along with its turbines.

In the Ruhr Valley, the weirs and mechanical plant at Echthausen and Wickede power stations had been totally destroyed. The weirs at Soest waterworks, Vereinigte Stahlwerke (steel works), and the power station at Frondenberg had been wrecked, and large portions of the neighbouring canal bank had caved in. More than five miles of overhead electric cables were also brought down in the area of Neheim and Frondenberg. Further afield, the waterworks dam at Gelsenkirchen had been completely destroyed, and at Dortmund the waterworks and power station were badly damaged, causing huge disruption to heavy industry and domestic supplies in the area.

Thanks to the floodwaters, the transport network and its infra-structure along the Möhne and Ruhr valleys also suffered badly. The main railway line from Hagen to Kassel was seriously damaged between Neheim and Wickede, and in places the track bed was completely washed away. At Wickede the track itself had been lifted bodily off the embankment and washed onto the lower lying fields below. It took until 11 June for express train services to be resumed. All road and narrow-gauge railway bridges in the Möhne Valley were destroyed by the power of the floodwaters, and damage to roads was severe, ranging from potholes to the complete destruction of the roadbed and metalling.

Industry in the Möhne and Ruhr valleys was hard hit by the attack. Numerous firms lost buildings, machinery and materials, swept away by the floodwaters or seriously damaged by mud, and they were also affected by damage to electricity and water supplies. The worst-hit area was the lower Möhne Valley around Neheim: the steel works at Hagen-Kabel and Harkort-Eicken in Wetter were extensively damaged by the effects of the attack.

Albert Speer recalled that his report on the situation, which he delivered to Hitler's headquarters soon after visiting the Ruhr Valley, 'made a deep impression on the Führer'.

Downstream from the Eder dam, the villages of Hemfurth, Affoldern, Mehlen, Bergheim and Giflitz were badly affected by the floodwaters, while several miles further on the Luftwaffe airfield at Fritzlar was completely flooded. Twenty-five road and rail bridges had

Below: A case of too little too late: barrage balloons fly over the Möhne in this German photograph taken late on 18 May.

been swept away, including the railway station at Giflitz and the bridge carrying the main line to Frankfurt. Serious inundations affected Hemfurth and Affoldern, as well as parts of the city of Kassel. In fact the effects of the flooding were felt in the Fulda and Weser rivers for a distance of about 300 miles from the Eder. At Hameln, more than 130 miles away, the River Weser rose by more than 20ft in the immediate aftermath of the raid.

As for the Sorpe dam, it withstood serious damage. 'They did achieve a direct hit on the centre of the dam,' wrote Speer. 'I inspected it that same day. Fortunately the bomb hole was slightly higher than the water level. Just a few inches lower – and a small brook would have been transformed into a raging river which would have swept away the stone and earthen dam.'

Initial claims of widespread loss of life among the population of the Ruhr Valley talked of between 3,000 and 4,000 dead, but this figure was soon refuted and the final death toll was eventually adjusted to 1,294, although some German sources believe it to be in excess of 1,400. Some 493 were Ukrainian women – forced labourers – although Dutch, French and Belgian prisoners of war were also among the casualties. Three months later, as the clearing up operation continued, bodies were still being found at Neheim.

Above: Flooding in the Eder Valley which resulted from the breach of the dam, and in particular the inundation of the Luftwaffe airfield at Fritzlar (seen here at centre), 15 miles south-south-west of Kassel. Hangars were flooded and the airfield was rendered completely unusable.
(IWM C5682)

Opposite: An incredible photograph taken at Neheim showing what remains of a detached house that stood in the path of the raging floodwaters from the Möhne. This house was lucky: many more were simply carried away by the floods and dashed to pieces.
(Bundesarchiv 1011/637/4193/20)

Above: A further view of the massive 230ft-breach in the wall of the Eder dam, probably photographed in the late afternoon of 17 May. Water pours through the breach at the rate of some 1.8 million gallons per second.

(RAF Museum PC71/19/795)

By noon on the 17th the floodwaters in the Ruhr Valley had abated in Neheim and Wickede, but the valley itself had been shorn of all its familiar features by the scouring effect of the fast-moving floodwaters. In their place had been left mounds of twisted debris, heaps of mud, metal girders, uprooted trees, furniture and personal belongings. Surprisingly, it was only a few days before water supplies had been fully restored in Neheim and its environs.

Shortly before the raid, water production in the Ruhr stood at one million cubic metres. Although this figure plummeted by three-quarters in its aftermath, within six weeks the original output had been restored. Water supplies to the city of Dortmund fell to one-fifth in a matter of hours after the raid: within three days they were back up to four-fifths.

Electricity supplies were also only temporarily disrupted. It was not necessary to rebuild the power station at the Möhne and the giant power plant at Herdecke was only offline for a fortnight. In any case, the Germans obtained alternative electricity supplies from generating stations that used water from the Alps.

At first sight, heavy industry appeared to have been largely unaffected: steel production in the Greater Reich and the occupied territories actually exceeded that of 1942 by 2.5 million tons.

In some respects, however, the attacks did have far-reaching effects on other parts of the Ruhr Valley's industrial infrastructure. The important waterworks at Frondenberg and Echthausen were disabled in the early hours of the 17th and were not returned to full working order until August. Official German records show that only a basic level of water supply to consumers was maintained in the aftermath of the attack.

The Ruhr suffered an 8 per cent reduction in steel output in the second half of 1943, while the whole of north-west Germany lost 1.9 million tons of crude steel production that year. Allied air raids over the region caused a significant loss in production of crude steel, with over 600,000 metric tons lost in May and June alone. This is particularly noteworthy, since only in four other months that year did lost production exceed 100,000 tons, with the highest figure reaching 137,000 tons.

The loss of vital water supplies to coke works in the Ruhr Valley also meant that supplies to principal gas consumers were slashed by more than half on 19 May.

Rebuilding of the Möhne and Eder dams proceeded quickly under the auspices of Albert Speer and the Todt Organisation, and on 25 September the yawning gap in the Möhne's wall was finally closed, while work on the Eder was completed soon afterwards. Both reservoirs were then able to hold water from the rainfall of winter 1943-4, but due to the extensive damage suffered by both dams the level of water in the reservoirs, including the Sorpe, was reduced accordingly as a precaution. It was not until 1946-7, when further repairs were carried out, that they were able to operate at full capacity once more.

Below: The Eder dam photographed from a Luftwaffe reconnaissance aircraft shortly after the attack.

(Crown Copyright)

Civilians in the Ruhr Valley queue for drinking water
in the aftermath of the dams raid.
(Bundesarchiv 101I/637/4193/20)

Above: By 10am on 17 May, the floodwaters of the Eder lake had reached the town of Kassel, 37 miles downstream, where the River Fulda rose to more than 13ft above its usual level.

(Crown Copyright)

Opposite: In these views of the Eder dam taken soon after the end of the war, the parapet walling has still to be replaced (above), while the repairs to the dam wall itself (below), completed in September 1943, have failed to reinstate numbers 3, 4 and 5 vents. However, final reconstruction was not completed until June 1944.

(Both pictures TRL Ltd)

Nor was it only industry that suffered the consequences of the attacks. Agriculture and food supplies were hit too. The scouring effect of the floodwaters stripped away topsoil on farmland in the Möhne and Eder valleys, rendering them virtually impossible to cultivate, and they remained barren for many years to come. Loss of agricultural production in the region could not quickly be made good by supplies from elsewhere in Germany because of the widespread disruption to communications caused by Allied air raids.

The diversion of labour and resources to repair the damage caused by the raids was short-term in its effects, but the need to build and man defences at dams considered liable to future air attack represented a longer-term drain on both civilian and military resources. Some 10,000 regular troops from the Heer and Luftwaffe, plus many more from reserve units, were diverted to this task from important duties elsewhere in the Reich.

The question of how best to protect Germany's dams from future air attack occupied the minds of Nazi officialdom for many months after the raids. At the Möhne dam, the results included additional torpedo nets, special Luftwaffe fighter cover, 328ft-high aerial steel curtains stretched across the reservoir to deter low-flying aircraft, and anti-bomb and anti-rocket netting projecting out from the wall on the dam's air side. This was in addition to searchlights, barrage balloons and smokescreen equipment. Extensive provision for the defence of the Eder and Sorpe dams was also made.

Repairs to the Möhne dam were completed on 25 September 1943, some eleven weeks after work had begun on 9 July.

(TRL Ltd)

Main picture: The Sorpe dam was a difficult nut to crack, mainly due to its concrete and earth core construction, and in the end it defied the RAF's attempts to breach it. However, the two Upkeep mines that were dropped succeeded in damaging the parapet structure (seen towards the centre of the wall). This led to a certain amount of water spillage from the reservoir into the compensating basin below the wall, which can be discerned from the stirred up sediment.

(IWM C5897)

Special bomb deflectors were built on the Möhne lake to create an underwater barrier that would prevent bombs from coming into contact with the dam wall. On the far left can be seen the curtain of anti-torpedo netting.

(TRL Ltd)

Above: Steel netting was erected on the valley side of the Möhne dam wall to deflect bombs. The twin towers were also reduced in height to prevent them from being used as markers again in an aerial attack.

(TRL Ltd)

But what of the civilian populations of the Ruhr and Eder valleys? The effect of the attacks on their morale is difficult to gauge. Allied bombing of the Ruhr had been going on for many years, with particular intensity between March and July 1943 in the so-called Battle of the Ruhr, during which time the RAF mounted thirty-one major raids. It is therefore difficult to separate the effects of the general bombing of the region from the specific civilian response to the dams raids. Much clearing up and rebuilding of homes had to be undertaken in the aftermath of the floods, but civilian wrath was not simply confined to Britain and the RAF.

The competence of the Luftwaffe was called into question since defensive measures to protect the dams was so obviously lacking. Indeed, the mayor of Essen, Julius Dillgardt, who was also Chairman of the Ruhr Valley Dams Association, had been involved in protracted correspondence with the military authorities since the beginning of the war regarding the protection of the Ruhr dams from air attack. The risk of a devastating attack on the dams from the air was still considered an impossibility by the military. Only the Möhne was linked to the Luftwaffe air defence system and no smoke generators were deployed at any of the dams until after the attack. Events were to prove that it was a prime example of blinkered thinking by the Nazi military authorities, and of shutting the stable door after the horse had bolted.

Jugendherberge Körbecke

Gruß vom schönen Möhnesee

Möhnetalsperre, Luftbild

Auf der Sperrmauer

Blick zur Sperrmauer

Albert Speer later wrote that: 'While we were engaged in rebuilding, the British air force missed its second chance. A few bombs would have produced cave-ins at the exposed building sites, and a few fire bombs could have set the wooden scaffolding blazing.'

However, for German Intelligence, something quite unexpected came out of the raids – an intact Upkeep mine, which they were able to successfully defuse. This was the weapon from F/L Bob Barlow's Lancaster, AJ-E, which had crashed at Haldern-Herken after hitting a high-tension electricity pylon. The mine had rolled clear of the blazing wreckage, relatively undamaged, and the self-destruction charge failed to go off. It was successfully defused and removed to a weapons evaluation depot at Kalkum near Dusseldorf for a thorough examination. From information obtained by the weapons experts at Kalkum and the interrogation statement of P/O Fraser, one of only two men to survive from Hopgood's crew, the Luftwaffe came close to uncovering the secrets of Barnes Wallis's bouncing bomb. By September 1943, the Germans were carrying out basic tests on a design for their own bouncing bomb weapon at the Luftwaffe's Ballistics Institute and Technical Academy at Berlin-Gatow. But the critical detail they failed to discover was the depth at which the bomb was supposed to explode, and that it had to explode in contact with the dam wall.

British fears that their attacks on the German dams could be

Above: By the 1950s the Möhne dam and lake had almost returned to normal.

Overleaf: A series of enhanced defensive measures were taken in Britain to defend its dams against a similar attack from the Luftwaffe. This is Graig Goch dam in the Elan Valley near Rhayader, not far from the Nant-y-Gro dam which was used by Barnes Wallis in his early trials for Upkeep.

Above: In this postwar photograph of the Eder dam, the repaired section of wall can be clearly seen in the left foreground. On the horizon is Waldeck Castle, which dominates the Eder reservoir.

(Richard Simms)

Opposite above: A wintry view of the Möhne dam, pictured from the Soest side of the lake in the 1990s.

(Richard Simms)

Opposite below: The Eder dam and lake seen in the late 1990s.

(Eder-Touristic Gmbh)

replicated by the Luftwaffe against dams in England and Wales led to enhanced defensive measures being taken at home, but the half-expected raids did not materialise. Speer himself wondered why the Luftwaffe didn't launch similar pinpoint attacks against key industrial targets in Britain. He raised this matter with Hitler at the end of May 1943, but the Führer appeared uninterested, commenting that the Luftwaffe's commanders would not be receptive to advice from Speer's industrialist advisers. In any case, he had already discussed this matter with General Oberst Jeschonnek (Göring's second-in-command) on several occasions, but they had failed to reach a decision. Once again, Hitler had thrown away a golden opportunity to do real damage to Britain's war economy.

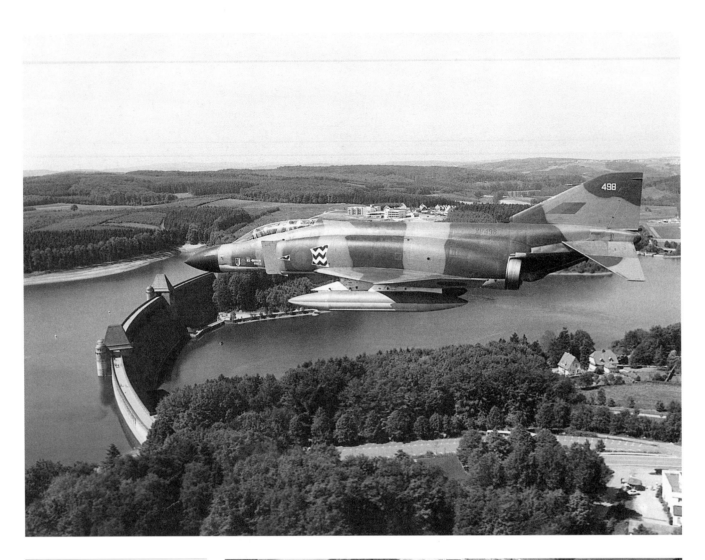

Above: A Phantom of 17 Squadron passes over the Möhne dam in 1974.

(RAF Germany)

Right: A postwar aerial view of the Möhne dam from the reservoir side, looking towards the compensating basin. The main power station below the dam wall that was destroyed by Hopgood's Upkeep has never been rebuilt.

(Bruce Robertson collection)

CHAPTER 7

THE AFTERMATH – BRITAIN

Harris, Cochrane and Wallis had followed the unfolding drama of the night in the tense atmosphere of the operations room at 5 Group HQ, Grantham. When they received the codeword 'Nigger' at 0056hrs, indicating that the Möhne dam had been breached, followed by 'Dinghy' at 0154hrs to confirm that the Eder too had been breached, there were scenes of intense jubilation in the ops room as the tension of the night's vigil suddenly evaporated. Wallis, who had paced nervously up and down and buried his face in his hands when each miss was reported, jumped for joy and threw his arms in the air. In his excitement, Cochrane jumped up and shook Wallis firmly by the hand. Harris grabbed the phone and asked to be put through immediately to Washington, where Churchill and the CAS Sir Charles Portal were attending the Trident Conference. At 0400hrs a car took Harris, Cochrane and Wallis to Scampton, where they joined the surviving crews of the first wave who were being debriefed.

Once debriefing was over, the crews retired to the mess for bacon and eggs and stood at the bar waiting for the others to arrive. But it eventually became clear that eight aircraft were missing and their crews would not be coming home. Wallis was becoming distressed over the high casualties suffered by the squadron and told Mick Martin if he'd known that so many aircrew were to die, then he'd never have embarked upon the project. Wallis had spent nearly 48 tense hours without sleep and was eventually persuaded to get some rest in G/C Charles Whitworth's house. But the party continued in the mess and around lunchtime transferred to Whitworth's house. Gibson had left early to help the adjutant, F/L Humphries, and 'Chiefy' Powell with the fifty-six casualty telegrams to next of kin. On the morning of the 18th,

APPENDIX 'G'
SPECIAL QUESTIONNAIRE

1. What could be seen of the objective during the run up? (With particular reference to the direction of the moon.)
2. At what range did you first see the target?
3. a) number and height of bounces of 'UPKEEP'.
    b) Was 'UPKEEP' spun? If so, what RPM?
4. Description of explosion, with particular reference to behaviour of the water, height of spout etc.
5. Description of damage to the target.
6. How many runs did you make?
7. Were you obstructed by any other aircraft during your run-up?
8. What method of control was used and was it effective?
9. What was the effect of the 100% night tracer carried
    a) on the enemy?
    b) on your own gunners?
10. Pilot's personal report (criticisms and comments).

APPENDIX 'G'
ANSWERS TO THE SPECIAL QUESTIONNAIRE
(Arranged in order of attack on each objective)

G/617   W/C Gibson   GO 939 Time of attack 00.28hrs
1. Saw the whole thing
2. 3-4 miles
3. (a) 3.
    (b) Yes, 500
4. Enormous column of water
5. There are two holes in the dam
6. One
7. No
8. VHF (perfect)
9. (a) Very satisfactory effect against gun positions. (b) No dazzle. Perfect for this job.
10. River below dam to a distance of about 3 miles was several times its normal size.

Note on GO 934 (Target Y, Eder)
1st and 3rd hit. 2nd overhit.
A large hole was definitely knocked in it and a great deal of water was seen flowing out.

Above: Safely home, but with adrenalin still pumping through their veins and the look of fatigue etched on their faces, Guy Gibson's crew are debriefed after the raid. As Bomber Harris and Cochrane look on, 617's intelligence officer, S/L Townson, unravels the hard facts behind the dramas of the night. From left to right: Harris, Townson, Spafford, Cochrane, Taerum, Trevor-Roper. *(IWM CH9683)*

the men of 617 Squadron went on some well-earned leave, three days for the ground crews, and seven for aircrew.

Meanwhile, across Britain the news of the raids came as a tremendous fillip to morale. The first reports of the operation were heard on the BBC radio news on the morning of the 17th, and the initial press coverage followed the same day in the regional evening newspapers. It was not until the 18th that the nationals went to town on coverage. 'RAF blow up three key dams in Germany' was the front-page headline in the *Daily Telegraph*, while the *Daily Herald* declared, 'RAF blows up dams with mines: 1,000 ft water spouts'. In a tone of excited triumphalism, the *Telegraph* went on to report:

With one single blow the RAF has precipitated what may prove to be the greatest industrial disaster yet inflicted on Germany in this war. A force of Lancasters, loaded with mines and with crews specially trained for the task, early yesterday morning attacked and destroyed the great dams on the Möhne

The Daily Telegraph
and Morning Post

No. 27,435   LONDON, TUESDAY, MAY 18, 1943   Printed in LONDON and MANCHESTER   PRICE 1½d.
4 A.M.

R.A.F. BLOW UP THREE KEY DAMS IN GERMANY

DEVASTATION SWEEPS DOWN RUHR VALLEY

BRIDGES AND POWER PLANTS ENGULFED

ADVANCING FLOODS STILL SPREADING FAST

With one single blow the R.A.F. has precipitated what may prove to be the greatest industrial disaster yet inflicted on Germany in this war.

A force of Lancasters, loaded with mines and with crews specially trained for the task, early yesterday morning attacked and destroyed the great dams on the Mohne and Sorpe rivers, tributaries of the Ruhr, and also the dam on the Eder River.

To-day walls of water sweeping down the Ruhr and Eder valleys are carrying everything before them.

The Air Ministry announced last night that a partial reconnaissance of the Ruhr Valley and the district near the Eder dam shows that the floods are spreading fast.

"The waters are sweeping down the Ruhr Valley," it stated. "Railways and road bridges are broken down. Hydro-electrical power stations are destroyed or damaged, a railway marshalling yard is under water.

"The floods from the breached Eder dam are already as great as the floods in the Ruhr Valley, but the country here is flatter and the water likely to spread over a greater area."

GERMANS ADMIT HEAVY CASUALTIES

The German communiqué yesterday, admitting that two dams had been "damaged"—it did not specify the area—said "heavy casualties were caused among the civilian population by the resulting floods." That was as much as the people of Germany were allowed to know. There was no reference to the disaster in later news broadcasts from Berlin.

The pilots, on their return, reported seeing in the moonlight huge breaches in the dams with water bursting through. They saw a power-station near the Mohne dam swept away in the flood and a 30ft high wall of water rumbling down the Eder valley.

Reporting personally to Air Chief Marshal Sir Arthur Harris, Chief of Bomber Command, Wing Cmdr. G. P. Gibson, who led the raid, said the immediate results of the destruction of the dams were far beyond their expectations.

Wing Cmdr. Gibson was the first to attack the Mohne Dam. After dropping his load he flew up and down drawing the enemy's fire to give the following planes a better chance of success. It was not until the fourth load had been dropped that the dam was first breached.

Air reconnaissance yesterday showed that there was a 100-yard gap in it.

There was no indication last night of the number of Lancasters engaged, but, although the loss of eight machines and their crews on an attack on such an objective must be regarded as fairly heavy, the complete success of the operation tells its own story of the worth of the sacrifice.

PARALYSING INDUSTRY

Apart from the cumulative damage caused by the floods, there is a firm reason for believing that the industry of the Ruhr will be partially paralysed by the destruction of the three dams.

All were full with the winter and spring rains. Even if repaired within a few months—if such a thing were possible—there would not be enough water to bring them into even partial use again until next spring. It took two years to fill the Sorpe reservoir, the smallest of the three, when it was first constructed.

Some idea of the flood of water released by the destruction of the dams can be judged from the fact that the 202,000,000 tons capacity of the Eder reservoir would have been enough to supply the whole of London for 150 days even in peace time.

The Eder reservoir, near Hemfurth, two miles south of Waldeck, is the largest in Germany. It had a surface area of 4½ square miles.

Its main purpose was to prevent flooding in the Weser and Fulda Valleys in winter and maintain the rivers at navigable depth in summer. It was also used to feed the Weser and Weser Canal and to operate several important power stations.

Kassel, 30 miles below the dam, is mostly low-lying, and its important locomotive works and aircraft factories are gravely threatened.

The half - mile - long Mohne Dam (and Sorpe Dam) lies about 26 miles east of the small manufacturing town of Dortmund, and was built before the last war to confine a reservoir six miles long by two miles wide and holding 134,000,000 tons of water.

It was the biggest source of water for the industries of the Ruhr, the demands of which are enormous. It was largely to meet the needs of the Ruhr's coke ovens and foundries that the dam was built.

The Sorpe Dam lies six miles south of the Mohne Dam, on the Sorpe River, also a tributary of the Ruhr. It was used in conjunction with the Mohne reservoir to control the Ruhr's supplies.

The DAILY TELEGRAPH Air Correspondent writes: "Were the mines dropped a little short the Lancasters were flying towards the dams their forward momentum would carry them against it—

(Continued on P. 6, Col. 4)

THE MOHNE DAM AFTER THE R.A.F. RAID

PILOT SEES BREACH IN DAM BY MOONLIGHT

SUCCESS AT FOURTH ATTEMPT

The full official account of the raid on the dams in South-West Germany was given by the Air Ministry last night in the following statement:

For many weeks picked Lancaster crews had been training for one operation. They worked in secrecy on a bomber station which, as far as possible, was cut off from any contact with the outside world.

HE DREW THE ENEMY'S FIRE

Only about half a dozen other men in the whole of Bomber Command knew what they were doing.

In the early hours of yesterday morning, when the weather had at length were exactly right, they carried out the operation. Its purpose was to subject the whole Ruhr valley to almost as severe an ordeal as it had undergone by fire in the last three months, and to do the same to other industrial areas farther east.

These picked men, under the command of Wing Cmdr. G. P. Gibson, D.S.O. and bar, D.F.C. and bar, went out to attack three huge water barrage dams. Two of them were on the rivers Mohne and Sorpe, tributaries of the River Ruhr, and the other on the River Eder.

The effects of both flood and shortage of water might be disastrous.

There are 300 and more waterworks and many pumping stations in the Ruhr valley. Interference with

(Continued on P. 6, Col. 3)

DISASTROUS EFFECTS
Hitting Ruhr Industry

The Mohne and Sorpe dams control 70 per cent. of the water catchment area of the Ruhr Basin. Before they were built the Ruhr was always apt to run short of water in a dry season—the Sorpe reservoir alone takes two or three years to fill.

If the reservoirs were suddenly emptied the floods that resulted would be as serious as the subsequent shortage of water. The pilot said that there must have been at least 100 enemy fighters up. The bombers

POWER PLANT BOMBED

Other bombers pounded the harbour installations and power supply at Lorient and submarine pens at the adjacent base of Kerman. The power plant at Lorient contains the transformers essential for the entire dock area.

Visibility was perfect and returning crews described the bombing results as excellent. One pilot said that there must have been at least 100 enemy fighters up. The bombers

ENEMY CONVOY ATTACKED

Coastal Command with considerable damage to Caen airfield and escorting Spitfires shot down five German fighters. These were the loss of one. Two more enemy planes were shot down in other operations.

BORDEAUX IS WITHOUT GAS OR WATER

LIBERATORS POUND U-BOAT BASES

The U-boat bases at Bordeaux, Lorient and Kerenan, all on the Atlantic coast of France, were the targets for a large number of American bombers in daylight yesterday. Four heavy and 10 medium bombers are missing.

Vichy radio stated last night that 148 people were killed and 228 injured at Bordeaux. Reports from Paris said that the town was without electricity, gas and water.

It was announced by American Army H.Q. last night that the attack on Bordeaux was made by a heavy force of Liberators. Their round trip was about 1,000miles.

Brig.-Gen. J. P. Hodges, commanding a Liberator wing, said it was the first time the Liberators had attacked in force. The bombing was good.

Rouen, which is one of the great harbours in the world, has a docking area of seven miles. It is now used chiefly as a U-boat building and outfitting centre.

Pilots described "bombing pattern" as good. The enemy, they said, was "caught flat-footed. There was little fighter or flak opposition."

TWO BLOCKADE RUNNERS SUNK IN ATLANTIC

SCUTTLED BY NAZI CREWS

Cruiser patrols of the Royal Navy have intercepted two more blockade runners bound for Germany and heavily laden with cargoes from the Far East. The enemy vessels were scuttled themselves after interception.

An Admiralty communiqué stated last night that one of them, the German armed ship Silvaplana, 4,793 tons, carried a valuable cargo of rubber and tin.

The entire ship's company of the Silvaplana, including more than 100 personnel of the German navy, were rescued by H.M.S. Adventure.

PANIC FOLLOWS SUMMONS

The other blockade-runner, the German motor vessel Regensburg, 8,068 tons, was intercepted between Greenland and Iceland by H.M.S. Glasgow (Capt. E. M. Evans-Lombe), patrolling in the Denmark Strait. She was brought-to with warning shots.

Signs of panic were immediately apparent on board the Regensburg. A number of her company being seen to jump over the side. The enemy then signalled, "I stop," and H.M.S. Glasgow ceased fire.

(Continued on P. 6, Col. 6)

U-BOATS STILL CHECKED

COL. KNOX'S COMMENT
From Our Own Correspondent
BOSTON, Monday.

Col. Knox, Secretary of the Navy, stated at his Press conference here to-day that "generally the picture is improving for the United Nations in submarine warfare, although it is subject to ups and downs."

"March, he said, was very bad. April was a good month, and May had been satisfactory so far.

"The Navy," he continued, "has by no means reached its peak. There will be twice as many ships in use at the end of 1943 as at the end of 1942. Every type of vessel is increasing ahead of schedule."

The number of aircraft-carriers, he added, would also increase many times by the end of the year compared with the end of 1942.

Initiative With Allies

Addressing the Boston Advertising Club at luncheon to-day Col. Knox said: "Whether we go east or west, north or south, the initiative now is in Allied hands."

"When war broke out," he added, "the United States was wondering when the Axis was going to strike next. Come what may now it will be the Allies who will strike, not the Axis."

MR. MACKENZIE KING GOES TO WASHINGTON

FROM OUR OWN CORRESPONDENT
WASHINGTON, Monday.

Mr. Mackenzie King, the Canadian Prime Minister, left Ottawa to-day for Washington for conferences with Mr. Churchill and Mr. Roosevelt.

Mr. Churchill and the President resumed their talks at the White House to-day. In accordance with Mr. Roosevelt's request to the Press to "put the lid on" news of these discussions over the week-end, nothing further can be said about the Prime Minister's appointments during the past two days.

According to reports from London a newspaper (not THE DAILY TELEGRAPH) has suggested that the United Nations' commander for the invasion of Europe has already been chosen, and that Gen. Alexander would be the logical choice. One Washington newspaper reproduces this report under the headline, "One Vote for Alexander."

Message to Stalin

President Roosevelt, it was disclosed at the White House to-night, has told M. Stalin that it is "reasonable to expect further success on both the Eastern and the Western fronts." He has also expressed the hope to Gen. Chiang Kai-shek that the Allied forces will take the initiative in Asia "in the near future."

TWO ALERTS IN LONDON

An Alert was sounded in London last night, the second in succession. A few enemy aircraft were reported and there were some bursts of gunfire.

The Raiders Past signal was sounded shortly afterwards. Night fighters were up.

A bomb dropped in a London suburb, damaged two houses and trapped their occupants, one of whom was feared dead.

Nearly two hours later London had a second Alert. [P6.]

R.A.F. ATTACK BASE 15 MILES FROM ROME

HANGARS LEFT IN FLAMES

FEEBLE GROUND DEFENCES

From W. E. MUNDY.
Daily Telegraph Special Correspondent
ALLIED H.Q., NORTH AFRICA, Monday.

British Wellington bombers of the North-West African Air Force flew over Rome last night, but dropped no bombs on the city.

They had none to drop. The target for all their bombs was the Italian seaplane base at Lido di Roma, 15 miles south-west of the capital, a few minutes earlier.

So bright was the moon that over Lido di Roma the Wellingtons were able to employ tactics usually associated with speedy daylight fighter-bombers. One made four separate runs over the target, the last being at only 750ft above the ground.

Other Wellingtons, having dropped their bomb loads, swept in twice at altitudes of between 400ft and 500ft to machine-gun planes lined up in front of hangars.

Pilots reported that the burning hangars looked like frameworks of twisted steel.

Axis opposition from ground defences was almost non-existent, and no enemy fighter put in an appearance during the whole trip.

Lido di Roma is close to the ancient anchorage of Ostia, at the mouth of the Tiber. It is connected with Rome by a fine highway built by Mussolini's orders.

Our bombers as they swept over Rome could see the buildings of the blacked-out capital clearly in the moonlight. The Colosseum and the Via Imperiale were easily recognisable.

GASWORKS BLOWN UP

On Saturday night our Wellingtons were over Trapani, in Western Sicily, and members of the crews reported that there was a huge explosion in the centre of the town. Some of the hits were observed near the railway station and barracks.

During daylight yesterday Coastal Air Force planes patrolling the coasts of Sardinia, Corsica, Sicily, and South-West Italy damaged and shot down a Ju.52 off the coasts of Bone, Algeria, and destroyed it.

R.A.F. long-range fighters attacked an enemy schooner off the east coast of Greece in daylight yesterday. The vessel was abandoned by its crew and the blaze was last seen listing badly. One smaller enemy sailing ship was also attacked and damaged.

From these and other operations four of our aircraft are missing.

ITALIAN CROWN PRINCE'S ROLE

CIANO SEES POPE
MADRID, Monday.

Crown Prince Umberto has taken the place of King Victor Emmanuel at meetings of the Supreme War Council in Rome since the downfall of the Axis in North Africa, according to reports from good sources reaching Madrid.

There is great political activity in the capital, with lengthy consultations between the King, Crown Prince and Mussolini.

Ciano, recently appointed Minister to the Vatican, is reported to have had a meeting with the Pope.

The recent heavy bombings of such towns as Palermo, in Sicily, and Civitavecchia, near Rome, have caused what is described in reports reaching Madrid as "considerable indignation and consternation."—R.U.P.

Rome Cabinet in Non-Stop Session. [P6.]

U.S. PIT TRUCE EXTENDED

FROM OUR OWN CORRESPONDENT
NEW YORK, Monday.

Mr. Lewis, president of the United Mineworkers' Union, has given an assurance that the 15-day coal truce which expires to-morrow night will be extended until the end of the month.

This followed an appeal made by Mr. Harold Ickes, Solid Fuels Secretary of the Interior, that work should continue. In this way, he said, "the path will be opened for immediate collective bargaining."

Earlier to-day, the War Labour Board issued a statement on Mr. Lewis's decision not to obey the Board's instruction to attend a meeting to arrange for a renewal of bargaining.

The issue, said the War Labour Board, was "whether Mr. Lewis is above and beyond the laws which apply to all other citizens of the United States." The statement accused Mr. Lewis of "defying the established procedure of the Government," and so "giving aid and comfort to our enemies."

BOMBER C.-in-C.'s PRAISE

"A MAJOR VICTORY"

Air Chief Marshal Sir Arthur Harris, C.-in-C., Bomber Command, has sent the following message to the Air Officer Commanding the Bomber Group whose Lancasters attacked the dams in Germany yesterday:

"Please convey to all concerned my warmest congratulations on the brilliant successful execution of last night's operations.

"To all the crews I would say that their keenness and thoroughness in training and their skill and determination in pressing home their attacks will for ever be an inspiration to the Royal Air Force.

"In this memorable operation they have won a major victory in the battle of the Ruhr, the effects of which will last until the Boche is swept away in the flood of final disaster."

COAL EMERGENCY IN CANADA

MR. KING'S WARNING
OTTAWA, Monday.

Mr. Mackenzie King, the Canadian Prime Minister, told the House of Commons to-day that a national emergency had been declared to exist in the production of coal in Canada.

An order is expected in a few days to compel men with coal mining experience to take employment in mines. Canada faces the possibility of being 4,000,000 tons short of her coal requirements next year.—A.P.

This Morning's War News

Germany
Devastation spreading down Ruhr and Eder valleys after destruction by Lancasters of Mohne, Sorpe and Eder dams; pilots' accounts. (Pp 1 & 6)

Italy
R.A.F. over Rome after moonlight raid on air base. (P1)

France
Heavy day raids on Bordeaux docks and Lorient. (P1)

Sea
Two blockade runners, trapped by Navy, scuttle themselves. (P1)
Atlantic air cover against U-boats now extends almost from port-to-port. (P6)

United States
Mr. Mackenzie King goes to Washington for Churchill-Roosevelt talks. (P1)
Resumption of pit strike threatened as 15-day truce ends. (P1)

Combined Operations
Four hundred Germans killed when destroyer Campbeltown was blown up at St. Nazaire raid. (P3)

Labrador
Allies huge new air base. (P5)

Tunisia
Navy seizes island off Cap Bon. (P5)

Marshal Messe
Italian C.-in-C. in North Africa arrives in Britain. (P6)

Russia
Russians shelling Seysk, on south-western base of Germans' Orel salient. (P5)

Black-out (London) 10.33–5.19
Moon rises 7.58 p.m.

ATTU BATTLE SATISFACTORY

From Our Own Correspondent
WASHINGTON, Monday.

The Navy Department, in one of its shortest communiqués of the war, announced to-night that "operations against the Japanese on Attu Island, in the Aleutians, are continuing."

No further details were given, but Col. Knox, Secretary of the Navy, said in Boston to-day that "the battle was moving along satisfactorily."

The only other indication of Attu progress was a radio talk last night by a War Department spokesman, Col. Ernest Deguy.

He said that operations were going according to plan on Attu, and that Kiska was next on the agenda.

Earlier to-day Tokyo radio quoted a Japanese army spokesman as saying that the attacking United States forces were landing a steady stream of reinforcements on the island under cover of naval and air bombardment.

GEN. QUINAN

Gen. Sir Edward Pellew Quinan, who was given the command of the new Tenth Army based in Iraq and Persia in February last year, has been appointed to the command of the North-Western Army in India.

He succeeds Gen. Sir Cyril Moves, who says Reuter, has been compelled to go on leave on account of ill-health.

LATE NEWS

LONDON ALERTS
(See Late Page.)
Raiders passed sounded some time afterwards. Later third Alert was sounded.
Enemy aircraft were over South-East England. High-explosive bombs dropped at one coastal town.

"ITALIAN CHIEF OF STAFF RESIGNS"
Moscow radio last night quoted Berne reports that Gen. Ambrosio, Chief of Italian General Staff, had handed resignation to Mussolini, who had asked him to withhold it until the draft had been reorganised.

ROOSEVELT MAY VETO TAX PLAN BILL
Washington, Tuesday.—President Roosevelt is hinting strongly at a veto if Congress approves the modified Income Tax Plan ("Pay As You Go") Bill, which has been approved by the Senate.
He declared that he could not acquiesce "in the elimination of whole year's tax burden on upper income groups during a war period."—A.P.

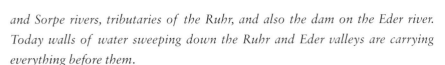

and Sorpe rivers, tributaries of the Ruhr, and also the dam on the Eder river. Today walls of water sweeping down the Ruhr and Eder valleys are carrying everything before them.

To a blitz-weary nation with little in the way of good news to celebrate since the British victory at El Alamein the previous autumn, this daring raid by RAF Bomber Command deep into the Nazi heartland struck a chord. Post-raid reports and the use of a dramatic photo-reconnaissance picture of the yawning breach in the Möhne dam on the front pages of national newspapers boosted public morale. Obtained at great personal risk by the RAF's high-flying PR Spitfire pilots from Benson, the benefits of selective use of such material as a highly effective propaganda tool soon became apparent to the British government.

News of the attacks provoked a favourable response from Britain's allies overseas, in Soviet Russia, the occupied countries of Europe and in particular the USA. Here it came at a timely point in the Trident Conference, and was widely and positively reported in the media. Up to this point, there were many in North America who had been expressing doubts about the effectiveness of Bomber Command's campaign, as

Below: Outside the officers' mess at Scampton the surviving captains from the raid are caught on camera. Back row, left to right: F/S Bill Townsend, F/L Joe McCarthy, F/L Harold Wilson (did not fly due to illness in his crew), W/C Guy Gibson, F/L Les Munro, F/L David Maltby, F/S Ken Brown. Front row, left to right: F/S Cyril Anderson, P/O Geoff Rice, F/L Harold 'Mick' Martin, F/L David Shannon, P/O Les Knight.
(RAFM P18734)

Above: Gibson with an almost complete line up of 617 Squadron aircrew pictured after the raid (possibly following their investiture on 22 June 1943).

(RAF Museum P4447)

well as that of their own 8th Air Force. Chastise gave Churchill the propaganda coup he was looking for, and just at the right time.

To 617 Squadron, Operation Chastise was not without its cost in human terms. The operation claimed the lives of fifty-three men, many of whom, like Hopgood, Maudslay and Young, were – even at the tender ages of 21, 21 and 27 respectively – highly experienced bomber pilots and impossible to replace. Sgt Jack Liddell from Weston-Super-Mare, who was the rear gunner in the crew of F/L Robert Barlow (AJ-E), was the youngest RAF fatality of the operation. At 18, he must have concealed his true age when he enlisted in 1941.

On 24 May, details of the decorations awarded to 617 Squadron's aircrew were passed on to the squadron, before they were officially announced in the supplement to the *London Gazette* the next day. Gibson received the Victoria Cross: Bomber Harris telephoned him to personally congratulate him on his award. Thirty-three members of the squadron were awarded gallantry decorations in recognition of their

THE AFTERMATH—BRITAIN

part in Chastise, making 617 the most decorated squadron in the RAF.

The publicity that followed the raid continued unabated, and on the 27th the King and Queen paid a Royal visit to Scampton, lunching in the officers' mess before being taken on a tour of inspection of aircraft and crews of both 57 and 617 Squadrons. The King also inspected one of 617's Lancasters, complete with Upkeep, and talked to Gibson and several other aircraft captains about their training for the raid and the attack itself.

On 21 June, 617's members travelled to London for their investiture by the Queen (the King was in North Africa) at Buckingham Palace the following day. On the evening of the 22nd, a celebratory dinner was held by A.V. Roe & Co. Ltd, builders of the Lancaster, at the Hungaria Restaurant in Lower Regent Street. In addition to 617 Squadron members, Roy Chadwick, designer of the Lancaster, Barnes Wallis and other personalities from Vickers were also present. The occasion was memorable for many reasons, not least for the fact that the food and

Overleaf: With a scale model of the Möhne dam and two potential designs for the badge of 617 Squadron before him, the King shares a joke with Gibson while Cochrane and Whitworth look on. *(IWM CH9924)*

161

The publicity that followed the raid continued
unabated, and on 27 May the King and Queen
visited Scampton to review 617 Squadron's air
and ground crews. With Lancaster G for George
as a backdrop (Gibson's aircraft on the raid),
Gibson escorts the King.
(IWM CH9950)

Opposite: Guy Gibson stands crisply to attention
for the inspection of 617 Squadron by the King and
Queen.
(IWM TR1002)

Above: Canadian survivors of the dams raid. Of the twenty-nine who took part in the operation, thirteen were killed and one became a PoW. Standing, from left to right: Sgt Stefan Oancia (AJ-F), Sgt Frederick Sutherland (AJ-N), Sgt Harry O'Brien (AJ-N), F/S Ken Brown (AJ-F), F/S Harvey Weeks (AJ-W), F/S John Thrasher (AJ-H), F/S George Deering (AJ-G) Sgt William Radcliffe (AJ-T), F/S Don MacLean (AJ-T), F/L Joe McCarthy (AJ-T), F/S Grant MacDonald (AJ-F). Front, Sgt Percy Pigeon (AJ-W), P/O Torger Taerum (AJ-G), F/O Danny (Revie) Walker (AJ-L), Sgt Chester Gowrie (AJ-H), F/O David Rodger (AJ-T).

(IWM CH9935)

drink on the menu were not subject to the usual rationing restrictions.

Guy Gibson achieved celebrity status in the months that followed, although to begin with he was something of a reluctant hero. Morale-boosting visits to war factories across Britain and rousing speeches at Wings for Victory parades were followed by an invitation from the Prime Minister himself, Winston Churchill, to accompany him to Canada for the Quebec Conference in August. After the conference, there followed a gruelling four-month-long public relations tour of Canada and the USA that saw Gibson attending civic receptions and making speeches at RCAF training airfields. Arriving back in England during December, his first instinct was to return to Scampton and look up his old oppos on 617 Squadron. But in his absence time had moved on. The squadron was now based at Coningsby and it had a new CO, W/C Leonard Cheshire. Gibson's hopes of being allowed to return to operations were dashed when 5 Group HQ officially grounded him and posted him away to a job at the Air Ministry in January 1944.

But the Guy Gibson story doesn't end there, as in the months that followed the hero was encouraged to write a book about his experiences as a bomber pilot, eventually to appear as *Enemy Coast Ahead* in 1946. Under the patronage of Winston Churchill, he was selected as the prospective Conservative parliamentary candidate for Macclesfield, but withdrew his candidacy in August, desperate to get back on operations. By now Gibson was an air staff officer at 54 Base and used his position to wangle his way back into operational flying. On 19/20 September 1944 he flew in a 627 Squadron Mosquito as master bomber on a raid against Rheydt and Mönchengladbach. His unfamiliarity with the Mosquito and the marking techniques employed proved to be his undoing, because on the way home his Mosquito crashed in Holland,

Overleaf. Australian survivors of the dams raid. Of the thirteen who took part in Chastise, two were killed. From left to right: F/L Bob Hay (AJ-P), P/O Lance Howard (AJ-O), F/L David Shannon (AJ-L), F/L Jack Leggo (AJ-P), P/O Fred Spafford (AJ-G), F/L Harold Martin (AJ-P), P/O Les Knight (AJ-N), F/S Bob Kellow (AJ-N). Not in this photograph are P/O Bert Foxlee and F/S Thomas Simpson who also survived the raid, and P/O Anthony Burcher who became a PoW.
(IWM CH9936)

During their investiture leave, five of 617's twelve
Australian aircrew are pictured in an informal pose
on the roof of the Admiralty building in London.
From left to right: Jack Leggo, Harold (Mick) Martin,
Tammy Simpson, Bob Hay and Bert Foxlee.
(IWM CH9943)

On 22 June, A.V. Roe & Co. hosted a celebratory dinner at the Hungaria Restaurant on Lower Regent Street in London to mark the investiture of 617's personnel by the Queen.
1) Sir Charles Craven, Chairman, Vickers-Armstrongs; 2) Sir Hew Kilner, Works Manager, Vickers-Armstrongs, Weybridge; 3) Air Cdre Charles Whitworth, OC RAF Scampton; 4) F/L Les Munro (AJ-W); 5) Capt H.A. 'Sam' Brown, Test Pilot, Avro; 6) F/L 'Capable' Caple, 617 Squadron engineering officer; 7) F/S Heveron ; 8) F/L Harold Wilson; 9) F/S 'Chiefy' Powell, flight sergeant i/c discipline, 617 Squadron; 10) F/L Dick Trevor-Roper (AJ-G); 11) F/O Edward Johnson (AJ-N); 12) F/O Harold Hobday (AJ-N); 13) F/L Harry Humphries, 617 Squadron adjutant; 14) P/O Don MacLean (AJ-T); 15) Capt Joe 'Mutt' Summers, Chief Test Pilot, Vickers-Armstrongs; 16) Barnes Wallis; 17) Sir Roy Dobson, Managing Director Avro; 18) P/O Lance Howard (AJ-O); 19) F/L Mick Martin (AJ-P); 20) F/L Jack Leggo (AJ-P); 21) Sgt Vivian Nicholson (AJ-J); 22) F/L David Maltby (AJ-J); 23) F/L Joe McCarthy (AJ-T); 24) W/C Guy Gibson (AJ-G); 25) F/S Len Sumpter (AJ-L); 26) P/O Toby Foxlee (AJ-P); 27) F/L Bob Hay (AJ-P); 28) F/S Tammy Simpson (AJ-P); 29) Roy Chadwick, Chief Designer, Avro; 30) Sir Frank Spriggs, Chairman, Glosters; 31) Sir Thomas Sopwith, Chairman, Hawker Siddeley.
(RAF Museum P4443)

172

An engaging studio portrait of Guy Gibson taken
after the dams raid.
(IWM CH13120)

Below: Pictured meeting the King at Scampton is F/L Joe McCarthy.

(IWM CH9925)

killing Gibson and his navigator, S/L J.B. Warwick. Exactly why they crashed is still a mystery. Perhaps the final words in the Guy Gibson story should be left to his biographer, Richard Morris: 'Gibson died not because he was sent back to battle, but because he refused to be left out of it.'

Following the dams raid, 617 Squadron went from strength to strength. With its reputation for precision bombing it continued to be employed on special bombing tasks until the war's end. Its Lancasters were further modified to carry Barnes Wallis's – 'super bombs' – the 12,000lb Tallboy and latterly the 22,000lb Grand Slam, which were used to breach the Dortmund-Ems canal, sink the much-feared German battleship *Tirpitz*, and bring down the Arnsberg viaduct, among many other operations. In the 21st century the legend of 617 Squadron lives on, with the Tornado instead of the Lancaster.

This page: The official citation for W/C Guy Gibson's Victoria Cross.

(PRO AIR2/4890)

CONFIDENTIAL.

RECOMMENDATION FOR IMMEDIATE AWARD.

Christian Names .....GUY PENROSE.......... Surname GIBSON,.DSO.&.Bar,.DFC.&.
Bar.

Rank .Squadron.leader.(Acting.Wing... Official No ..39438...........
Commander)

Command or Group 5.Group.Bomber.Command Unit ..617.Squadron...........

Total hours flown on operations :   1st Tour (Hampdens)   242.30
                                     2nd Tour (Fighters)NIGHT 199.45
                                     3rd Tour (Lancasters) 200.44

Recognition for which recommended .....Victoria.Cross,.............

Appointment held ....Officer Commanding, No. 617 (B) Squadron.

PARTICULARS OF MERITORIOUS SERVICE.

On joining Bomber Command in the early days of the War, this then junior Officer quickly established a reputation as an outstanding operational pilot.   Not content with taking the fullest possible share in all normal operations, he developed a habit of going out alone during his "rest" nights to make single-handed attacks on, for instance, such highly defended objectives as the German battle-ship "Tirpitz", then completing in Wilhelmshaven.   At the con-clusion of **his** first operational tour on night bombers, he persistently demanded to remain on operations.   He was, therefore, transferred to night fighters for his "rest" period, in preference to a training unit.   At that time the foundations of the night fighter organization were being laid, and this by then highly experienced night pilot took a leading part in raising and indoctrinating new night fighter formations.   During this period as a night fighter pilot, although stationed in a part of the country comparatively free from raids, and with night fighting tactics and equipment in the elementary stage, he destroyed at least three enemy bombers over this country.   At the conclusion of this tour as a night fighter pilot, he again insistently demanded to be returned to night bomber operations.   As a Squadron Commander his second operational tour on bombers was marked by consistently outstanding achievements, both as an operational pilot and as the leader of his squadron.   On the conclusion of this his third operational tour, he again raised the most strenuous protests against relegation to non-operational duties. He was therefore given command of a unit then forming for special tasks.   It was as the Commander of this unit that he led the attacks on the Moehne and Eder Dams.

It is typical of this Officer that he himself made the first attack on the Moehne Dam, thus taking the full brunt of the anti-aircraft defences while still at their best.   After delivering his attack with great accuracy from a height of a few feet, he proceeded to supervise the remainder of the attack on the Moehne Dam.   In the process he deliberately and repeatedly circled round at a very low altitude directly over the anti-aircraft defences for 30 minutes in order to attract their fire to his own aircraft and to enable his gunners to shoot up the gun positions, thus leaving the remaining aircraft, which were attacking the Dam in turn, as free as a run as possible.   After the Moehne Dam had been breached he withdrew the remainder of his force and led them to the Eder Dam.   Having already expended his own projectiles, he pursued similar tactics while the attack on the Eder Dam was successfully developed. Throughout both attacks he maintained a minute by minute commentary thus enabling reserve forces to be accurately disposed.

This young Officer is beyond doubt the most inspiring leader, efficient operational captain, and outstanding fighting airman of the Command.   Of a quiet and unassuming manner, and possessing an unfathomable store of personal courage, he displays all greatest qualities of leadership including intelligence and organizing ability of the highest order.   He is as insatiable in seeking the post of greatest danger as he is imperturbable in the encounter.

For extraordinary courage, exceptional leadership and example in the face of the enemy over three and a half years of hazardous operations culminating in the successful attacks on the Moehne and Eder Dams, which he personally led and wherein he displayed, as is usual with him, the highest valour in the face of deliberately sought and tremendous additional risk, this Officer is most strongly recommended for the award of the Victoria Cross.

This page: The official citation for F/S Ken Brown's award of the Conspicuous Gallantry Medal. It also includes citations for immediate awards of the Distinguished Flying Medal to Sgt Dudley Heal (navigator) and Sgt Stephen Oancia (bomb aimer) in Brown's crew.

(PRO AIR2/4967)

CONFIDENTIAL.

Canada

RECOMMENDATIONS FOR HONOURS AND AWARDS.

Surname: BROWN

Christian Names: KENNETH WILLIAM

Official No: R.94567.

Rank: FLIGHT SERGEANT

Unit: No. 617 Squadron.

Command or Group: No. 5 Group.

Total hours flown on operations: 44.20 hours.

Number of Sorties: 8.

Recognition for which recommended: C.G.M.

Appointment held: A Flight Sergeant of the R.C.A.F. employed as a Pilot in No. 617 Squadron.

Surname: HEAL

Christian Names: DUDLEY P.

Official No: 919764.

Rank: SERGEANT

Unit: 617 Squadron.

Command or Group: No. 5 Group.

Total hours flown on operations: 38.15 hours.

Number of sorties: 7.

Recognition for which recommended: D.F.M. (Immediate)

Appointment held: A Sergeant of the R.A.F.V.R. employed as a Navigator with No. 617 Squadron.

Surname: OANCIA

Canada

Christian Names: STEPHEN

Official No: R.114949

Rank: SERGEANT

Unit: No. 617 Squadron.

Command or Group: No. 5 Group.

Total hours flown on operations: 36.15 hours.

Number of sorties: 6.

Recognition for which recommended: D.F.M. (Immediate)

Appointment held: A Sergeant of the R.C.A.F. employed as an Air Bomber in No. 617 Squadron.

PARTICULARS OF MERITORIOUS SERVICE.

F/Sgt. Brown was Captain, Sgt. Heal Navigator and Sgt. Oancia Air Bomber of a Lancaster aircraft detailed to carry out an attack on the Sorpe Dam.

On arrival over the target, F/Sgt. Brown found that a thick fog had formed after the previous attack. Despite this, he flew around the target at low level, until there was a momentary clearance. By quickly making his run at the right time, and by a very high standard of crew co-operation, F/Sgt. Brown succeeded in dropping his mine in exactly the right position, in spite of adverse conditions.

This crew pressed home their attack with the utmost determination and have set an excellent example.

I strongly recommend that their outstanding achievement be recognised by the

-2-   Contd.Over.....2

immediate award of the Conspicuous Gallantry Medal to F/Sgt. Brown, and the immediate award of the Distinguished Flying Medal to Sergeant Heal and Sergeant Oancia.

Date:- 20th May, 1943.

Group Captain Commanding,
R.A.F. Station, Scampton.

REMARKS BY AIR OR OTHER OFFICER COMMANDING.

I concur in the above recommendations.

Opposite above and below: F/L David Maltby and F/L Harold (Mick) Martin meet the King at Scampton.

(IWM CH9929/CH9928)

178

OPERATION CHASTISE – AWARDS TO MEMBERS OF 617 SQUADRON

Clockwise: Victoria Cross, Distinguished Flying Medal ribbon, Conspicuous Gallantry Medal ribbon, Distinguished Flying Cross, Distinguished Service Order ribbon.

Victoria Cross

A/W/C G.P. Gibson DSO & Bar, DFC & Bar (OC 617 Squadron and Captain, AJ-G)

Distinguished Service Order

F/L J.C. McCarthy DFC (Captain, AJ-T)
F/L D.J.H. Maltby DFC (Captain, AJ-J)
A/F/L H.B. Martin DFC (Captain, AJ-P)
A/F/L D.J. Shannon DFC (Captain, AJ-L)
P/O L.G. Knight (Captain, AJ-N)

Bar to the Distinguished Flying Cross

A/F/L R.C. Hay DFC (Squadron Bombing Leader and B/A, AJ-P)
A/F/L R.E.G. Hutchison DFC (Squadron Signals Leader and W/Op, AJ-G)
A/F/L J.F. Leggo DFC (Squadron Navigation Officer and Nav, AJ-P)
F/O D.R. Walker DFC (Nav, AJ-L)

Distinguished Flying Cross

A/F/L R.D. Trevor-Roper DFM (R/G, AJ-G)
F/O J. Buckley (R/G, AJ-L)
F/O L. Chambers (W/Op, AJ-P)
F/O H.S. Hobday (Nav, AJ-N)
F/O E.C. Johnson (B/A, AJ-N)
P/O G.A. Deering (F/G, AJ-G)
P/O J. Fort (B/A, AJ-J)
P/O C.L. Howard (Nav, AJ-O)
P/O F.M. Spafford DFM (B/A, AJ-G)
P/O H.T. Taerum (Nav, AJ-G)

Conspicuous Gallantry Medal (Flying)

F/S K.W. Brown (Captain, AJ-F)
F/S W.C. Townsend DFM (Captain, AJ-O)

Bar to Distinguished Flying Medal

Sgt C.E. Franklin (B/A, AJ-O)

Distinguished Flying Medal

F/S G.A. Chalmers (W/Op, AJ-O)

F/S D.A. MacLean (Nav, AJ-T)

F/S T.D. Simpson (R/G, AJ-P)

F/S L.J. Sumpter (B/A, AJ-L)

Sgt D.P. Heal (Nav, AJ-F)

Sgt G.L. Johnson (B/A, AJ-T)

Sgt V. Nicholson (Nav, AJ-J)

Sgt S. Oancia (B/A, AJ-F)

Sgt J. Pulford (FE, AJ-G)

Sgt D.E. Webb (F/G, AJ-O)

Sgt R. Wilkinson (R/G, AJ-O)

Above: Trevor-Roper, Maltby, Gibson, Johnson, Martin, Shannon, Hobday and McCarthy are among this happy group of 617 Squadron members outside Buckingham Palace following their investiture.

(IWM HU62923)

C H A P T E R   E I G H T

SOME MEN WHO MADE IT HAPPEN

Below: Barnes Wallis, designer of the bouncing bomb.

(Via Bruce Robertson)

Sir BARNES WALLIS (1887–1979)

After the Second World War had ended, Barnes Wallis was awarded the sum of £10,000 for his bomb inventions – Upkeep, Tallboy and Grand Slam. He donated the money to establish an educational foundation for the children of RAF men killed on operations during the war.

The son of a doctor, Barnes Neville Wallis was born on 26 September 1887 in Ripley, Derbyshire. Educated at Christ's Hospital, Sussex, he went on to train as a marine engineer at J.S. White & Co. at Cowes on the Isle of Wight (1905) before being appointed as design draughtsman in the Airship Department of Vickers Ltd (1913). With the outbreak of the First World War, Wallis enlisted in the Artists' Rifles and was later commissioned into the Royal Navy Volunteer Reserve, but in 1916 he was sent back to Vickers to resume his airship design work. From 1923 to 1930 he was Chief Designer of the Airship Guarantee Company and with Sir Dennistoun Burney he worked on the R100 design. Wallis

Opposite: W/C Guy Gibson, commanding officer
of 617 Squadron on the Ruhr dams raid in 1943.
(IWM CH13121)

brought a fresh new approach to airship design that utilised his revolutionary 'geodetic' lattice construction principle in their construction. Progressing to heavier-than-air aircraft, Wallis employed geodetics in the design of the single-engine Vickers Wellesley in 1935 followed by the twin-engine Wellington in 1936.

From 1937 to 1945 Wallis was Assistant Chief Designer of the Aviation Section of Vickers-Armstrongs Ltd. With the outbreak of the Second World War his employers and the Air Ministry were keen that he should continue his work on aircraft design and development, but in his spare time he pursued a number of different ideas with which he hoped Britain could defeat the Nazis. Most famous of all his wartime inventions was the revolutionary bouncing bomb, used to great effect by 617 Squadron to destroy the Möhne and Eder dams in May 1943. Wallis also designed and developed the 12,000lb Tallboy and 22,000lb Grand Slam earthquake bombs that were used to sink the German battleship *Tirpitz* and to destroy vital strategic targets that included U-boat pens and V-weapon sites.

After the war, Wallis continued with his revolutionary designs for aircraft. During his research that began in 1945, he solved the difficult mechanical problem of altering the angle of wing sweep in flight to suit different conditions. Sadly, his ground-breaking work failed to attract the support of the British government and his designs were passed to the USA, and in the mid-1960s they were developed as the General Dynamics F-111 swing-wing bomber.

Wallis was made a CBE in 1943 and knighted in 1968. He was elected FRS in 1945 and was awarded the silver medal of the Royal Aeronautical Society in 1928 and 1937. Wallis maintained a close practical involvement with aviation right up until his death on 30 October 1979, at the age of 92.

Wing Commander GUY GIBSON (1918–44)

Alongside Leonard Cheshire, Guy Gibson is probably the most famous RAF bomber pilot of all time. Precocious, arrogant, and with an unrelenting enthusiasm for operations, he won undying fame for his role leading the attack on the Ruhr dams in May 1943, for which he was awarded the VC. Gibson flew operationally from the day war broke out, completing 177 operational sorties, with few breaks, until his final, fateful flight in September 1944.

Born on 12 August 1918 in Simla, the son of an official in the Imperial Indian Forest Service, Guy Penrose Gibson was educated at St Edward's School, Oxford, before being commissioned into the RAF in 1937. His first posting was to 83 Squadron as a bomber pilot. Gibson's early career in the junior service was undistinguished, but the war was to bring unforeseen change. Completing his first tour of duty in August 1940, he was posted to instruct at an operational training unit before transferring to Fighter Command and a posting to 29 Squadron flying

Bristol Beaufighter night fighter aircraft. In ninety-nine operational sorties Gibson claimed three enemy aircraft destroyed and was promoted to squadron leader with a bar to his DFC on completion of his second tour in December 1941. A short spell of instructing was followed by a posting back to Bomber Command and the command of 106 Squadron. He completed his second bomber tour in March 1943 as a wing commander aged 24, with DSO and Bar, DFC and Bar, before he was told to form 617 Squadron on 21 March. He led nineteen Lancasters on the famous dams raid on 16/17 May, in which the Möhne and Eder dams were successfully breached, but eight Lancasters failed to return. Gibson was awarded the VC and remained with the squadron until August, when he was officially taken off operations.

Thereafter and until D-Day, he became a celebrity figure at home and in the USA, a protégé of Winston Churchill, a prospective Conservative Party candidate for Macclesfield, and the author of what later became a best-selling account of the bomber air war, *Enemy Coast Ahead*. However, he was desperate to get back to operational flying and in September 1944 his superiors finally relented and granted him one final sortie. Gibson piloted a 627 Squadron Mosquito as master bomber in a raid on Rheydt and Mönchengladbach on 19 September. On the return journey his aircraft inexplicably flew into the ground and exploded, close to the Dutch town of Steenbergen, killing Gibson and his navigator, S/L James Warwick.

Flight Lieutenant 'MICK' MARTIN (1918–88)

'Mick' Martin was probably the RAF's greatest exponent of low-level bombing, and to those with whom he flew he was the greatest exemplar of low-flying skills, which were so well demonstrated in the dams raid of 1943. One commentator described him as 'swashbuckling and brave, with scant respect for authority, but with a compelling desire to be at grips with the enemy. But he was highly professional and knew that gallantry was no avail without skill and tactical sense.'

Born Harold Brownlow Morgan Martin at Edgecliff, New South Wales, on 27 February 1918, 'Mick' Martin was pronounced unfit to fly in Australia because of asthma. Undeterred, he worked his passage to England, where he joined the RAF in 1940. Martin was commissioned in 1941 and then served with 455 Squadron RAAF. He was transferred to 50 Squadron RAF, with whom he flew a further twenty-three sorties before being taken off operational flying and awarded the DFC. Chosen by Guy Gibson to join the newly formed 617 Squadron, Martin flew on the dams raid, for which he was awarded the DSO. Staying with the 'Dam Busters', he became its acting commanding officer and flew on many more dangerous operations until in February 1944 he was grounded by the AOC 5 Group. By this time he had been awarded bars to his DSO and DFC but was relegated to 'flying a desk' at group headquarters. Frustrated by this turn of events, he managed to inveigle his way back onto operations as the commander of 515 Squadron, flying de Havilland Mosquitos on night intruder and bomber escort sorties. Martin received a second bar to his DFC and by the war's end he had amassed a total of eighty-three sorties.

On 30 April 1947 he established a record for the flight from London to Cape Town when, flying a Mosquito with S/L E.B. Sismore as navigator, he covered the 6,717 miles in 21 hours 31 minutes at an average speed of 310mph.

He was granted a permanent commission in 1945 and enjoyed a highly successful postwar career, rising to high rank. He commanded the 2nd Allied Tactical Air Force and RAF Germany from 1967 to 1970 and retired from the RAF in 1974 as Air Marshal Sir Harold Martin KCB, DSO*, DFC**, AFC. He died on 3 November 1988.

Air Vice-Marshal The Hon Sir RALPH A. COCHRANE (1895–1977)

In the opinion of AVM Donald Bennett, the legendary commander of 8 (Pathfinder) Group, Cochrane was a disaster: 'He would have been the best group commander in Bomber Command had he done ten trips – or if he had done any trips. But his knowledge of flying and of operations was nil.' Objective truth, or simply the clash of two powerful personalities? Bomber Harris, however, had known Cochrane since before the war and regarded him as 'a most brilliant, enthusiastic and hard working leader of men'.

Below: Air Vice-Marshal the Hon Sir Ralph Cochrane, AOC 5 Group, RAF Bomber Command, 1943.
(IWM CH14564)

Born on 24 February 1895, Cochrane was educated at the Royal Naval Colleges at Osborne and Dartmouth before entering the Royal Navy in 1912, transferring to the RAF in 1918. A number of overseas postings culminated in 1936 with his appointment as the first Chief of the Air Staff to the Royal New Zealand Air Force. In 1942, Cochrane became AOC 3 Group Bomber Command, and with the sacking by Harris of AVM Alec Coryton in February 1943 he assumed the command of 5 Group. Cochrane had been a flight commander of a squadron commanded by Bomber Harris in Mesopotamia during the 1920s and as such remained a strong supporter of the C-in-C, a loyalty evidently reciprocated. Nevertheless, Cochrane was a difficult man to get along with and was viewed by many as austere and lacking in humour. He retired from the RAF as Vice-Chief of the Air Staff in 1952, and died in 1977, aged 82.

THE DAM BUSTERS

Below: Air Chief Marshal Sir Arthur Harris,
Commander-in-Chief RAF Bomber Command,
1942-5.

Air Chief Marshal Sir ARTHUR 'BOMBER' HARRIS (1892–1984)

Known widely by his nickname 'Bomber', but to his aircrews as 'Butch', Air Chief Marshal Sir Arthur Harris was the architect of Britain's strategic air offensive against Germany in the Second World War, and for three years he pursued the systematic destruction of the Third Reich with a single-minded determination. Of the Allied wartime commanders, Harris is arguably the most controversial, and to this day his name is closely linked with the questionable policy of area bombing. Although he did not invent area bombing, he applied himself rigorously to its execution, and demonstrated to the world the importance of strategic air power and the key role played by the RAF in the Allied war effort.

188

Harris was a man who expressed himself clearly and who exuded a definite sense of purpose, although he was seen by some as unrefined and rude, lacking in sensitivity, impatient and totally inflexible. Yet generally he was regarded with affection by his bomber crews, and with awe by his many minions at Bomber Command headquarters.

Although promoted Marshal of the RAF in 1945, unlike the other main leaders of the war years Harris did not receive a peerage in the 1946 New Year honours. Politicians, including Churchill himself, were quick to distance themselves from the bomber offensive once the war had been won, and Sir Arthur Harris and Bomber Command became victims of postwar political expediency.

Group Captain JOHN WHITWORTH (1912–74)

Born John Nicholas Haworth Whitworth in 1912 in Buenos Aires, he joined the RAF in 1930 and was appointed station commander at RAF Scampton in March 1942 as a group captain, DSO, DFC.

Capt JOSEPH J. 'MUTT' SUMMERS (1904–54)

Captain Joe 'Mutt' Summers was chief test pilot at Vickers-Armstrongs, Weybridge, from 1929 to 1951. 'All test pilots regarded him with some awe', wrote Britain's Concorde chief test pilot Brian Trubshaw. 'He was a great pilot who belonged to the "seat of the pants" vintage, a great character, full of humour, as well as being an excellent teacher who was always ready to pass on his vast experience.'

When Summers joined the RAF in 1920 on a short service commission, his abilities as a pilot were soon apparent and led to his posting to the A&AEE at Martlesham Heath in Suffolk, where he test-flew single-seat fighter aircraft. It was there that he acquired the nickname of 'Mutt', by which he became widely known for the rest of his life. In 1929 he was appointed Chief Test Pilot to Vickers and during the course of his service with the company he made more than forty maiden flights in prototype aircraft. On 6 March 1936, Summers played a key part in the birth of an aviation legend when he took up the prototype Spitfire on its maiden flight from the Supermarine airfield at Eastleigh.

During the Second World War he worked closely with Barnes Wallis, testing his bouncing bomb. On 3 December 1942 Summers flew a Wellington bomber for the first test drop of the mine off Chesil Beach on the Dorset coast. Unfortunately the results were not good because the mines shattered on contact with the water, but the trials continued and in January 1943 the weapon finally proved itself.

After the war Summers continued test-flying, and on the thirty-ninth anniversary of Blériot's cross-Channel flight he flew a Nene-engined Vickers Viking airliner from London to Paris in the record time of 34 minutes 7 seconds, at an average speed of 384mph. In 1951, after retiring from test-flying, he was for a year the liaison officer at the

Opposite: Dr William Glanville, Director of the Road Research Laboratory.

(The Royal Society/Godfrey Argent)

Weybridge Division of Vickers-Armstrongs. He was made an OBE in 1946 and a CBE in 1953. 'Mutt' Summers died at the relatively young age of 50, on 16 March 1954.

Dr D.R. PYE (1886–1960)

A keen musician and mountaineer, Sir David Randall Pye CB, FRS, MA, ScD, MIMechE, FRAeS, was born in London on 29 April 1886 and educated at Trinity College, Cambridge, where he read mechanical science. During the First World War he served in the RFC and latterly with the RAF as an Experimental Officer before returning to Cambridge in 1919 to become Fellow of Trinity College and lecturer in engineering. In 1925 Pye left the academic world to take up an appointment at the Air Ministry as Deputy Director of Scientific Research, a post he held until 1937, when he became Director. During the early war years he became closely associated with the development of the jet engine, but at the same time he also saw the potential in Barnes Wallis's research to develop an effective method of destroying dams. He offered Wallis his support in 1941, a critical time, sanctioning use of the Road Research Laboratory for a trials programme to assess the effects of explosive charges when placed against or near to a wall of a gravity dam. Pye was knighted in 1952 and was elected President of the Institution of Mechanical Engineers. He died on 20 February 1960.

Dr WILLIAM GLANVILLE (1900–76)

Outstanding both as scientist and director, Sir William Glanville CB, FRS, PhD, ScD, spent all his working life in the scientific civil service. A physically imposing man of commanding presence, he was not afraid to express his views clearly and firmly. Glanville was widely respected for his intellect and powers of judgement, as well as for his loyalty to his staff.

Born in London on 1 February 1900, the son of a builder, he was educated at Kilburn Grammar School and the University of London. He graduated in 1922 with a First Class Honours degree in civil engineering and began work as an engineering assistant at the newly formed Building Research Station, initially at Acton, and then at Garston near Watford. His main contribution in research was his early work on the properties of reinforced concrete, which ultimately formed the basis for a code of practice for the design of reinforced concrete structures.

When war broke out, he devoted the laboratory to the war effort, and it soon became an important centre of backroom research. Much work was undertaken into recording blast pressures from bombs and other munitions in air and water, and earth movements caused by buried bombs. Extensive use was made of scale models to investigate explosion phenomena as well as the effects on concrete of projectiles and shaped charges. The greatest of these scale-model investigations

was to determine the correct position and charges for the attacks on the Möhne and Eder dams.

Glanville was president of the Institution of Civil Engineers in 1950–1, elected FRS in 1958 and knighted in 1960 before he retired in 1965. He died on 30 June 1976.

Sir HENRY TIZARD (1885–1959)

Born on 23 August 1885, educated at Westminster and Magdalen College, Oxford, Henry Thomas Tizard joined the Royal Garrison Artillery on the outbreak of the First World War, transferring to the RFC the following year. By the end of the war he had become lieutenant-colonel and Assistant Controller of Experiments and Research for the fledgling RAF. Later, during the Second World War, in his role as Chairman of the Aeronautical Research Committee and

Scientific Adviser to the Chief of the Air Staff, his influence was vital in securing for Barnes Wallis the use of the shipping research tanks at the National Physical Laboratory in Teddington. Sir Henry Tizard GCB, AFC, FRS, died on 9 October 1959.

Air Marshal Sir CHARLES PORTAL (1893–1971)

A quiet and affable man, the 46-year-old 'Peter' Portal was still relatively young to succeed Sir Edgar Ludlow-Hewitt as C-in-C Bomber Command in 1940, but his prodigious intelligence and determination as a commander had singled him out for high office. Just six months into his command at High Wycombe he was appointed Chief of the Air Staff in October 1940, in which role he was later to become strongly committed to using Bomber Command in the fullest way possible to destroy Nazi Germany.

An authority on falconry and fishing, Charles Portal was born on 21 May 1893 and educated at Winchester and Christ Church, Oxford. He joined the Royal Engineers in 1914 and as a corporal was mentioned in despatches before receiving a commission and transferring to the RFC as an observer. By the end of the First World War he had risen to the rank of lieutenant-colonel, with a DSO and Bar and an MC. Between the wars his RAF career was meteoric and during his short spell at the helm of Bomber Command he steered it through the dangerous summer of 1940. He took office as Chief of the Air Staff that same year, where he remained for the duration of the war.

Portal was a member of the Chiefs of Staff Committee, in which capacity he played a full part in presenting to the Prime Minister and the War Cabinet the advice of the Chiefs of Staff on Allied strategy and other important matters of military policy. He was also present at all the wartime conferences of the Allied leaders, including Trident in Washington (where he was on the night of the dams raid). He died on 22 April 1971.

CHAPER NINE

A CINEMATIC LEGEND

MAKING THE DAM BUSTERS FILM

With the defeat of the Axis powers in 1945, six years of bitter fighting came to an end. A whole host of personal war stories were just waiting to be told, and it was not long before the first of the autobiographies by the RAF's wartime high commanders and squadron bosses hit the bookstalls. Wing Commander Guy Gibson's classic, *Enemy Coast Ahead*, was published posthumously in 1946 (spawning Paul Brickhill's equally good *The Dam Busters* in 1951), closely followed in 1947 by Marshal of the RAF Sir Arthur Harris's *Bomber Offensive* and Air Vice-Marshal Donald Bennett's *Pathfinder* (1958).

Not to be outdone, the film-makers made a significant contribution to the wartime lore of the RAF. Terence Rattigan's *The Way to the Stars* (1945) and Philip Leacock's *Appointment in London* (1953) highlighted on the big screen the part played by the men of Bomber Command during the war years. But, arguably, one of the most famous of all British war films must be *The Dam Busters*, combining stiff upper-lip performances, British design ingenuity and strong storyline in full measure.

Eleven years after the dams raid, 617 Squadron's remarkable exploit was turned into a blockbusting film by the Associated British Pictures Corporation (ABPC), starring Michael Redgrave as Barnes Wallis and Richard Todd as Guy Gibson. To this day it has remained one of the most enduring war films of all time, thanks in part to the understated way in which the story is told. But this was not the first time a film had been proposed about the raid: late in 1943 an American proposal to make a Hollywood movie about the dams raid was considered by the Air Ministry and the Ministry of Information. However, British reluctance to divulge specific operational details to the Hollywood

studio, not to mention strong criticism of the script from, among others, Barnes Wallis, meant the plan came to nothing.

The screenplay for ABPC's picture was by the famous British playwright R.C. Sherriff, author of *Journey's End* and the screenplay for the movie *The Invisible Man*. It was based on the first half of Paul Brickhill's best-selling book, *The Dam Busters*, and on a part of Gibson's own account in *Enemy Coast Ahead*. Michael Anderson, who was relatively unknown in the film world at the time, was picked to direct the film. It was his first major picture, although he was later to win acclaim for directing *The Quiller Memorandum*, *Around the World in Eighty Days* and *Logan's Run*. He chose to approach the story in a documentary style and to film it in monochrome, thereby giving the story a hard-edged grittiness that colour stock would have failed to do. It also enabled original film footage of bouncing bomb test drops made during the war to be seamlessly inserted into the new feature film. When Eric Coates was approached to write the title theme, he replied, 'I think I finished it yesterday'. In fact, he had already written a suitable work, and his rousing 'Dam Busters March' became one of the best-known pieces of film music ever written. It made the Top Ten in 1955, remained there

Opposite: Cinema poster advertising Michael Anderson's *The Dam Busters*.

(Canal+Image)

Above: Inspirations for a cinema epic: Guy Gibson's *Enemy Coast Ahead* (1946), and Paul Brickhill's *The Dam Busters* (1951).

for more than a year and was even arranged as a hymn tune.

To make the film as accurate as possible, when work on the script began in earnest, drafts were sent to aircrew survivors of the dams raid for their comments. Expert technical advice was also on hand from Barnes Wallis himself (he paid many visits to Elstree Studios during the film's production), as well as from 'Bomber' Harris, the Hon. Sir Ralph

Cochrane (AOC 5 Group in 1943), Mick Martin (skipper of P for Popsy) and Group Captain J.N.H. Whitworth (station commander at Scampton in 1943).

For many, the star of the film is undoubtedly the Avro Lancaster itself. It is hard to believe that Lancasters were in short supply in April 1954 when filming commenced at RAF Scampton, but four Mk 7

Above: Upkeep was still on the secret list when *The Dam Busters* was made, and it remained so until 1963. For the purposes of the film, an accentuated representation of the bouncing bomb was fabricated and bolted to the underside of the Lancasters. Also visible in this photograph are the cut-away bomb bay and absence of mid-upper turret.

(Canal+Image)

aircraft were taken out of storage from 20 Maintenance Unit, Aston Down, and specially modified for the film: these were NX673, NX679, NX782 and RT686. In fact, '673, 679 and 782 had already developed a taste for the movies because they had recently starred in Philip Leacock's feature film about a wartime Lancaster squadron, *Appointment in London*, which was premiered in 1953.

In common with the actual Lancaster B Mk I (Type 464 Provisioning) that flew on the dams raid in 1943, three of the Mk 7s (NX673, NX679 and RT686) had their mid-upper gun turrets and bomb bay doors removed to convert them to the authentic dam buster configuration. The bomb bay itself was further modified to create the rebated aperture from which the mock-up of the bouncing bomb was suspended. However, the bomb itself was still on the secret list when the film was being made, so the resulting mock-up bore little resemblance to the real thing.

Michael Redgrave as Barnes Wallis, during filming at the National Physical Laboratory's Ship Tank at Teddington, where tests for the bouncing bomb were re-created for the film.

(Canal+Image)

The aircraft wore different squadron code letters on each side of the fuselage, thereby enabling three Lancasters to play the parts of six on screen. NX679 was painted to represent Guy Gibson's ED932 AJ-G, and it was the only aircraft to have its serial number altered for the film. The other Lancasters retained their official RAF serials. NX673 was painted in the markings of Mick Martin's P for Popsy. One Lancaster, NX782, was retained as a standard Mk 7, and painted as ZN-G to represent Gibson's aircraft when he served with 106

Squadron, before being called upon to form 617 Squadron.

Another aircraft that had a 'walk-on' role in the film was Vickers Wellington T10, MF628, which appears briefly in the early part of the film on a test air-drop of the mine. Because her appearance on screen was short, it was decided to keep MF628 in her silver Training Command livery instead of repainting her in the standard wartime night bomber camouflage of black, dark green and dark earth. At the time of filming in 1954, MF628 was the only flying example of the

When *The Dam Busters* was filmed at RAF Scampton in 1954, the station had changed little since the war. Here, 617's crews are filmed leaving from the actual building at Scampton where the final operational briefing took place in 1943. *(Canal+Image)*

During training for the actual dams raid, Henry Maudslay returned from a low-level training sortie with foliage caught on the underside of his Lancaster. Here, Richard Todd as Guy Gibson, Nigel Stock (Fred Spafford) and Brewster Mason (Dick Trevor-Roper) look on as a similar scene is re-created during filming.

(Canal+Image)

Above: Harbingers of destruction: Lancasters stand bombed-up and ready for take-off in the film.
(Canal+Image)

Wellington extant, and today she can still be seen on static display at the RAF Museum, Hendon.

The RAF put Scampton aerodrome at the disposal of ABPC for location work, and a spell of good weather meant filming could proceed unhindered. Avro Lincoln crews from the nearby RAF base at Hemswell flew the Lancasters on camera and were led by a former fighter 'jock' named Ken Souter. Under the control of director of photography Erwin Hillier, much of the superb aerial footage was filmed by ABPC's second unit team from a loaned RAF Vickers Varsity, as well as from cameras placed inside the Lancasters themselves. To facilitate filming, the metal floor of the Varsity was replaced by a wooden one, to which were attached camera tripods and grips. The aircraft's nose section was also modified to take a forward-looking camera. A further two cameras were installed inside the aircraft, one beside the rear port side passenger access door and the other in the left-hand seat of the cockpit, the pilot flying from the right-hand seat.

Flying sequences showing the early tests of the bouncing bomb were shot off the shoreline at Skegness in Lincolnshire because it was near to the main filming activity at Scampton. The practice flights before the raid, and the actual bombing runs over the dams during the raid itself, were filmed over Lake Windermere in the Lake District and at the Derwent reservoir and dam in the Derbyshire Peak District. In fact, the latter was one of three dams actually used by 617 Squadron in April and May 1943 for intensive flying training before the raid. Scenes of the Lancasters crossing the 'enemy coast' were probably shot over Gibraltar Point near Skegness, or near Southwold in Suffolk. The scenes of inundation in the Ruhr Valley that appear towards the end of the film were photographed in 1954 when the area of the dams itself fell victim to a natural flood disaster. Michael Anderson sent a film unit to Germany especially to capture this event for incorporation into the final version of the film.

Once the location filming had been completed at Scampton, the unit moved to ABPC's studios at Elstree in Hertfordshire, where the set builders and model makers had been hard at work. The office interiors for Bomber Harris, Gibson and Wallis had been recreated, as well as a number of interiors at Scampton and the 5 Group operations room. Although the real 5 Group underground operations room at Grantham had been sealed up at the end of the war, by a stroke of luck it had remained untouched since then, its contents frozen in time. ABPC had discovered this fact and were allowed in to photograph this remarkable time capsule, thereby enabling them to recreate a faithful studio mock-up for the film.

For the various scenes depicting action inside the Lancasters, ABPC constructed mock-ups at Elstree of the various crew stations, as well as installing a complete Lancaster nose section mounted on a moving platform. The cockpit controls were linked to a motor beneath the platform to create a kind of basic flight simulator. When the control column was moved the platform moved too, creating a realistic flying movement of the aircraft nose section on screen.

During the long spells of filming in the studio, Richard Todd was strapped into the pilot's seat in the nose section for hours at a time while scenes were shot and shot again until the director was happy with the result. To help pass the time in between 'takes', Todd was taught by an RAF flying instructor how to 'fly' the platform correctly, learning how to operate a Lancaster up to take-off speed. For the purposes of the film, he had to be seen starting up and taxiing, and on occasions he actually piloted a Lancaster on its take-off run at speeds of up to 70mph. Sadly for Todd, he then had to throttle back the engines and return to the dispersal.

Overleaf: Richard Todd as Guy Gibson reveals to his pilots that they have been training for a precision attack on the Ruhr dams. He is pointing at the actual three-dimensional model of the Möhne dam and lake that was made by the RAF's CIU at Medmenham for 617 Squadron's operational briefing in 1943.

(Canal+Image)

211

To simulate the explosions of the bouncing bombs and the dam walls crumbling away under the massive back-pressure of water, it was important to recreate authentic scale models of the dams and their lakes in the studio. Three accurate mock-ups of the dams and surrounding countryside, measuring 300ft long by 150ft wide, filled the entire sound stage at Elstree. Camera tracks and a swinging arm for the high-speed camera were also added to facilitate filming.

It took ten months of filming before the picture was finally 'in the can' and post-production work could commence. The film then had to be edited, special effects incorporated and the sound track added.

Demand for tickets to see the première of *The Dam Busters* was so great that two Royal Performances were held in London. The first showing on 16 May 1955 – the twelfth anniversary of the raid – was attended by Princess Margaret. Also present were some of the surviving aircrew from the dams raid, including Mick Martin (skipper AJ-P), Harold Hobday (navigator AJ-N) and Bert Foxlee (front gunner AJ-P), as well as Guy Gibson's father, and his widow, Eve. The second performance on the following night was screened in the presence of the Duke and Duchess of Gloucester.

Once filming had been completed, in October 1954 the four Lancasters that helped to recreate the epic story were returned to the RAF maintenance unit at Aston Down, where they languished until declared surplus to requirements. Without ceremony, they were sold to the British Aluminium Co. in July 1956 and melted down for scrap.

To this day the film *The Dam Busters* remains a classic of its kind and a fitting memorial to the achievements of Barnes Wallis, Guy Gibson and the gallant men of 617 Squadron. However, it is sad to report that for reasons of political correctness, a television showing of *The Dam Busters* by ITV in June 2001 saw all references to Guy Gibson's black Labrador dog, 'Nigger', expunged from the film. When challenged on the matter, a spokesman for ITV said that the word 'nigger' was offensive and that they didn't want to upset viewers. It is a fact that the word 'nigger' is offensive to many people in the 21st century, but the film and Guy Gibson's decision to name his dog as he did were products of their time – a different world with a different set of values. This rewriting of history to suit the mood of the day is a dangerous road to go down, and one cannot help but ask just how far we should go in distorting historical fact to conform to the whim of the moment.

Thankfully, there were people during the Second World War years who were prepared to speak frankly, defend freedom of speech and even sacrifice their lives; certainly, without such sacrifice, the rewriting of history to suit political ideology would have become commonplace in the totalitarian society that a Nazi-dominated Britain would have become.

Previous page: Richard Todd as Guy Gibson is told that his black Labrador dog, Nigger, has been run over and killed outside the camp gates.

(Canal+Image)

Opposite: 'Gentlemen. Your target for tonight will be the great dams of western Germany.'
Richard Todd, with Ernest Clark as Cochrane and Derek Farr as Whitworth.

(Canal+Image)

THE DAM BUSTERS (length 11,230ft) Cert 'U'

The Cast

Barnes Wallis	Michael Redgrave
Mrs Wallis	Ursula Jeans
Doctor	Charles Carson
Sir David Pye	Stanley van Beers
Dr W.H. Glanville	Colin Tapley
Committee members	Frederick Leister, Eric Messiter, Laidman Brown
Official, National Physical Laboratory	Raymond Huntley
Official, Ministry of Aircraft Production	Hugh Manning
Capt Joseph (Mutt) Summers	Patrick Barr
Observers at trials	Edwin Styles, Hugh Moxey
RAF officer at trials	Anthony Shaw
Air Chief Marshal Sir Arthur Harris	Basil Sydney
Air Vice-Marshal the Hon. Ralph Cochrane	Ernest Clark
G/C J.N.H.Whitworth	Derek Farr
Farmer	Laurence Naismith
Group signals officer	Harold Siddons
BBC announcer	Frank Phillips

Members of 617 Squadron

W/C Guy Gibson	Richard Todd
His crew:	
F/L R.D. Trevor-Roper	Brewster Mason
F/L R.E.G. Hutchison	Anthony Doonan
F/O Spafford	Nigel Stock
F/L A.T. Taerum	Brian Nissen
F/S J. Pulford	Robert Shaw
P/O G.A. Deering	Peter Assinder
S/L H.M. Young	Richard Leech
S/L H.E. Maudslay	Richard Thorp
F/L J.V. Hopgood	John Fraser
F/L W. Astell	David Morell
F/L H.B. Martin	Bill Kerr
F/L D.J.H. Maltby	George Baker
F/L D.J. Shannon	Ronald Wilson
F/O L.G. Knight	Denys Graham
F/L R.C. Hay	Basil Appleby
F/L J.F. Leggo	Tim Turner
F/S G.E. Powell	Ewen Solon
W/C Gibson's batman	Harold Goodwin

Credits

Director in charge of production	Robert Clark
Based on	*The Dam Busters* by Paul Brickhill and W/C Gibson's *Enemy Coast Ahead*
Screenplay	R.C. Sherriff
Director of photography and aerial photography	Erwin Hillier
Art director	Robert Jones
Special effects photography	Gilbert Taylor
Production manager	Gordon Scott
Editor	Richard Best
Casting directors	Robert Lennard, G.B. Walker
Assistant director	John Street
Camera operators	Norman Warwick and Val Stewart
Sound recordist	Leslie Hammond
Dubbing editor	Arthur Southgate
Continuity	Thelma Orr
Make-up	Stuart Freeborn
Hairdresser	Hilda Winifred Fox
Technical adviser	G/C J.N.H. Whitworth
March, 'The Dam Busters'	Eric Coates
Music score	Leighton Lucas
Performed by	The Associated British Studio Orchestra
Musical director	Louis Levy
Recording director (RCA Sound)	H.V. King
Production supervisor	W.A. Whittaker
Directed by	Michael Anderson
Made at	Associated British Studios, Elstree, England
World distribution	Associated British-Pathé

Overleaf: The cover of the souvenir programme produced for *The Dam Busters*.

(Canal+Image)

ASSOCIATED BRITISH PRESENTS

Richard TODD · Michael R

THE DA

WITH

URSULA JEANS · BASIL SYDNEY · PATRICK BARR · E

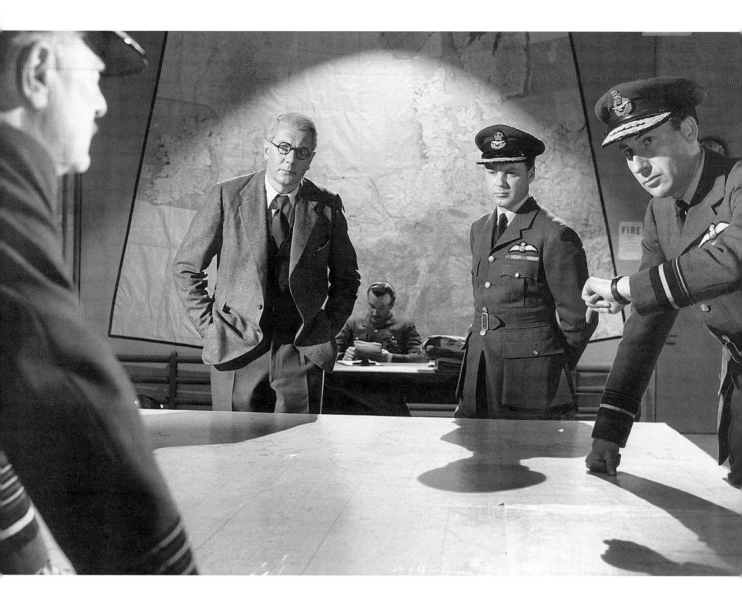

Above: Inside 5 Group's operations room at Grantham, the tension mounts as Operation Chastise reaches its climax. The ops room was accurately recreated for the film from photographs and plans of the original building. Left to right: Basil Sydney as Harris, Michael Redgrave (Wallis), Derek Farr (Whitworth), and Ernest Clark (Cochrane).

(Canal+Image)

THE AIRCRAFT IN THE FILM
AVRO LANCASTER
Built in 1945 by Austin Motors, Longbridge, as B Mk VIIs

NX673

Sept 1945	–	Issued to 32 MU (RAF St Athan)
Nov 1945	–	To 9 Squadron, RAF Waddington
Jan 1946	–	To India for photo survey work
Apr 1946	–	Returned to UK. Stored at 20 MU (RAF Aston Down)
Mar 1950	–	To 5 MU (RAF Kemble)
Apr 1950	–	Returned to 20 MU
May 1952	–	Issued out for film work at RAF Upwood (*Appointment in London*)
Jul 1952	–	To 20 MU
May 1954	–	To RAF Hemswell for filming (*The Dam Busters*)
Oct 1954	–	Returned to 20 MU and declared non-effective stock
Jul 1956	–	Scrapped

NX679

Jul 1945 — To 617 Squadron RAF Waddington

Oct 1945 — Issued to 32 MU

Jan 1946 — To India

May 1952 — Returned to UK and stored at 20 MU, issued out for film work at RAF Upwood (*Appointment in London*)

Jul 1952 — Returned to 20 MU

Sept 1953 — Transferred to non-effective stock

May 1954 — To RAF Hemswell for filming (*The Dam Busters*)

Oct 1954 — Returned to 20 MU and declared non-effective stock

Jul 1956 — Scrapped

NX782

Oct 1945 — Unspecified ground accident, Cat Ac

Mar 1946 — With Air Command South East Asia, probably with Tiger Force

May 1946 — Issued for return to UK

May 1952 — Issued out for film work at RAF Upwood (*Appointment in London*)

Jul 1952 — Held at 20 MU

Mar 1954 — To RAF Hemswell for filming (*The Dam Busters*)

Oct 1954 — Returned to 20 MU and declared non-effective stock

Jul 1956 — Scrapped

RT686

Issued to 32 MU

Feb 1946 — To RAF Swinderby

Mar 1946 — To 15 MU (RAF Wroughton)

Sept 1953 — Transferred to non-effective stock

Mar 1954 — To RAF Hemswell for filming (*The Dam Busters*)

Oct 1954 — Issued to 20 MU and declared non-effective stock again

Jul 1956 — Scrapped

VICKERS WELLINGTON

Built in 1944 as a B Mk X by Vickers (Blackpool)

MF628

May 1944 — Issued to 18 MU, RAF Tinwald Downs

Mar 1948 — Converted to T10 by Boulton Paul, Wolverhampton

Apr 1949 — To No 1 Air Navigation School, RAF Hullavington

Dec 1951 — Accidental damage (Cat 4), but repairable

Oct 1952 — To 19 MU RAF St Athan

Apr 1954 — To RAF Hemswell for use in filming of *The Dam Busters*

1955 — Sold to Vickers-Armstrongs, Weybridge

1956 — Presented to Royal Aeronautical Society

1972 — On permanent loan to RAF Museum

1981 — Returned to original B Mk X configuration

(Histories compiled by Trevor Green, RAF Museum, and the author)

Overleaf: Mission accomplished. Richard Todd (Gibson) and his crew on arriving back at Scampton after Operation Chastise. Lancaster Mk 7, NX679, was the only aircraft to have its serial altered for the film when it was painted to represent Guy Gibson's Lancaster, ED932/AJ-G. NX679 had also featured in another film about a wartime Lancaster bomber squadron, *Appointment in London*, in 1952.

(*Canal+Image*)

BIBLIOGRAPHY

DOCUMENTS
Public Record Office, Kew
AIR 2/4890   Award Citation for A/W/C Guy Gibson
AIR 2/4967   Award Citation for F/S Ken Brown

BOOKS
Air Publication 2062A, *Pilot's and Flight Engineer's Notes: Lancaster I, III and X* (Air Ministry, 1944)

Babington-Smith, Constance, *Evidence in Camera* (London, Chatto and Windus, 1958)

Brickhill, Paul, *The Dam Busters* (London, Evans, 1951)

Chorley, W.R., *RAF Bomber Command Losses of the Second World War 1943* (Leicester, Midland Counties Publications, 1996)

Dictionary of National Biography, 1951–60, 1971–80

Euler, Helmuth, *The Dams Raid Through the Lens* (London, Battle of Britain International, 2001)

Falconer, Jonathan, *Bomber Command in Fact, Film and Fiction* (Stroud, Sutton, 1996)

Gibson, Guy, *Enemy Coast Ahead* (London, Michael Joseph, 1946)

Hastings, Max, *Bomber Command* (London, Michael Joseph, 1979)

Leaf, Edward, *Above All Unseen: The RAF's Photographic Reconnaissance Units 1939–1945* (Sparkford, PSL, 1997)

Lumsden, Alec, *Wellington Special* (Shepperton, Ian Allan, 1974)

MacBean, John A., and Hogben, Arthur S., *Bombs Gone: The development and use of British air-dropped weapons from 1912 to the present day* (Wellingborough, PSL, 1990)

Mason, Francis K., *The Avro Lancaster* (Bourne End, Aston Publications, 1989)

Morris, Richard, *Guy Gibson* (London, Viking, 1994)

Nesbit, Roy Conyers, *Eyes of the RAF: A History of Photo-Reconnaissance* (Stroud, Sutton, 1996)

Speer, Albert, *Inside the Third Reich* (London, Weidenfeld & Nicolson, 1970)

Sweetman, John, *The Dambusters Raid*, 2nd (revd edn) Edition (London, Jane's, 1990)

Tubbs, D.B., *Lancaster Bomber* (London, Pan/Ballantine, 1972)

Journal and Magazine Articles

'The Dam Busting Weapon', Dr B.N. Wallis, *Air Clues*, May 1963

'The Origins and Design of the Attack on the German Dams', A.R. Collins, *Proceedings of the Institution of Civil Engineers*, Pt 2, June 1982, Vol. 73

'Photography of the Dams', *Coastal Command Quarterly Review* (n.d., *c.* 1943)

'The Dams Raid and After', Alfred Price, *Purnell's History of the Second World War*, Vol. II, No. 10

'The Ruhr Dams Raid 1943', *After the Battle*, No. 3, 1973

'Dam Busters: The Film', François Prins, *FlyPast*, October 1985

'The Last Dambuster', Jack Meadows, *Aeroplane Monthly*, May 2000

Newspaper Obituaries

The Times, 17 March 1954, Joseph 'Mutt' Summers

Daily Telegraph, 31 October 1979, Sir Barnes Wallis

The Times, 4 November 1988, Sir Mick Martin

Daily Telegraph, 22 October 1990, Sir Ben Lockspeiser

The Times, 28 September 1998, Joe McCarthy

Websites

www.cwgc.org – The Commonwealth War Graves Commission, Debt of Honour Register

www.bundesarchiv.de – Bundesarchiv

www.iwm.org.uk – Imperial War Museum

www.rafmuseum.org.uk – RAF Museum

APPENDIX I

FAILED TO RETURN

Eight 617 Squadron crews failed to return from the dams raid, representing the loss of fifty-six aircrew, of whom only three men survived to become prisoners of war. The circumstances of each aircraft loss are recorded below, and the individual aircrew names that follow include details of rank, decorations, age, and home town (where known) at the time of death. Also included are details of the three prisoners of war and the three aborted sorties.

THE CASUALTIES

Hopgood crew

AJ-M, ED925/G damaged by flak on its approach to Möhne dam, then caught in the blast from its Upkeep weapon which had overshot the parapet and exploded on the air side of the dam. Crashed at 0034hrs at Ostonnen, 3¾ miles east of Werl, Germany.

F/L John Vere Hopgood DFC and Bar, RAFVR, 21 (Seaford, Sussex)
Sgt John William Minchin RAFVR, 27 (Bedford)
Sgt Charles Brennan RAFVR
F/O Kenneth Earnshaw RCAF
P/O George Henry Ford Goodwin Gregory DFM, RAFVR

Young crew

AJ-A, ED877/G shot down by flak crossing the Dutch coast on the return flight, and crashed at 0258hrs off Castricum-aan-Zee, Holland.

S/L Henry Melvin Young DFC and Bar, RAFVR, 27
Sgt David Taylor Horsfall RAF, 23 (Hove, Sussex)

Sgt Lawrence William Nichols RAFVR, 33 (Westgate, Kent)

F/O Vincent Sanford MacCausland RCAF, 30 (Prince Edward Island, Canada)

Sgt Gordon Arthur Yeo RAFVR, 20 (Barry Dock, S. Wales)

Sgt Wilfred Ibbotson RAFVR, 29 (Bretton West, Yorks)

F/S Charles Roberts RAFVR

Maudslay crew

AJ-Z, ED937/G badly damaged over the Eder dam by the detonation of its own Upkeep weapon and hit by flak on the return flight. Crashed at 0236hrs at Netterden, 1¼ miles east of Emmerich, Germany.

S/L Henry Eric Maudslay DFC, RAFVR, 21 (Broadway, Worcs)

Sgt John Marriott DFM, RAFVR, 23 (Chinley, Cheshire)

F/O Robert Alexander Urquhart DFC, RCAF

WO2 Alden Preston Cottam RCAF, 30 (Jasper Park, Alberta)

P/O Michael John David Fuler RAFVR, 23 (West Wickham, Kent)

F/O William John Tytherleigh DFC, RAFVR, 21 (Hove, Sussex)

Sgt Norman Rupert Burrows RAFVR

Astell crew

AJ-B, ED864/G flew into high-tension cables and pylon on the outward flight near Marbeck, 3 miles SSE of Borken, Germany. Crashed at 0015hrs.

F/L William Astell DFC, RAFVR, 23 (Manchester)

Sgt John Kinnear RAF, 21 (East Newport, Fife)

P/O Floyd Alvin Wile RCAF, 24 (Truro, Nova Scotia)

WO2 Abram Garshowitz RCAF

F/O Donald Hopkinson RAFVR, 22 (Royton, Lancs)

F/S Francis Anthony Garbas RCAF

Sgt Richard Bolitho RAFVR, 23 (Portrush, Co. Antrim)

Barlow crew

AJ-E, ED927/G flew into high-tension cables on the outward flight at Haldern, 2 ½ miles ENE of Rees, Germany. Crashed at 2350hrs.

F/L Robert Norman George Barlow DFC, RAAF, 32 (St Kilda, Victoria)

P/O Samuel Leslie Whillis RAFVR, 31 (Fenham, Newcastle-upon-Tyne)

F/O Philip Sidney Burgess RAFVR, 20

F/O Charles Rowland Williams DFC, RAAF, 34 (Torrens Creek,
    Queensland)
P/O Alan Gillespie DFM, RAFVR, 20 (Carlisle)
F/O Harvey Sterling Glinz RCAF, 22 (Winnipeg,
    Manitoba)
Sgt Jack Robert George Liddell RAFVR, 18
    (Weston-super-Mare, Som)

Byers crew
AJ-K, ED934/G hit by flak on the outward
flight from batteries on the Dutch island of
Texel and crashed into the Waddenzee west of
Harlingen (precise time unknown).

P/O Vernon William Byers RCAF, 32 (Codette,
Saskatchewan)
Sgt Alastair James Taylor RAF, 20 (Alves, Moray)
F/O James Herbert Warner RAFVR
Sgt John Wilkinson RAFVR, 21 (Antrobus, Cheshire)
P/O Arthur Neville Whitaker RAF
Sgt Charles McAllister Jarvie RAFVR, 21 (Glasgow, Scotland)
F/S James McDowell RCAF

Ottley crew
AJ-C, ED910/G hit by flak on the outward flight and
crashed on the Boserlagerschenwald near Hessen,
1¾ miles NNE of Hamm, Germany, at 0235hrs.

P/O Warner Ottley DFC, RAFVR
Sgt Ronald Marsden DFM, RAF, 23 (Redcar,
Yorks)
Sgt Harry John Strange RAFVR, 20 (Holloway,
London)
F/S Thomas Barr Johnston RAFVR
(Bellshill, Lanarks)
Sgt Jack Guterman DFM, RAFVR, 23 (Guildford, Surrey)
F/O Jack Kenneth Barrett DFC, RAFVR, 22 (Goodmayes, Sussex)

Burpee crew
AJ-S, ED865/G hit by flak on the outward flight and crashed at 0200hrs
near Gilze-Rijen airfield, Holland.

P/O Lewis Johnstone Burpee DFM, RCAF, 25 (Ottawa, Ontario)
Sgt Guy Pegler RAF, 21 (Bath, Som)
Sgt Thomas Jaye RAFVR, 21 (Crook, Co. Durham)
P/O Leonard George Weller RAFVR, 28 (Harpenden, Herts)

WO2 James Lamb Arthur RCAF, 25 (Coldwater, Ontario)
Sgt William Charles Arthur Long RAFVR, 19 (Bournemouth, Hants)
WO2 Joseph Gordon Brady RCAF, 27 (Ponoka, Alberta)

THE PRISONERS OF WAR

P/O Jim Fraser RCAF (AJ-M) – Stalag Luft 3, Sagan and Belaria
P/O Anthony Burcher DFM, RAAF (AJ-M) – Stalag Luft 3, Sagan and Belaria
Sgt Fred Tees (AJ-C) – Stalag Luft 6, Heydekrug

THE ABORTED SORTIES

F/L Les Munro
AJ-W, ED921/G hit by light flak on the outward flight crossing Vlieland, Holland, damaging the VHF radio and intercom. Landed back at Scampton 0030hrs with mine still onboard.

F/O Geoff Rice
AJ-H, ED936/G hit the sea on the outward flight near Vlieland, ripping off the Upkeep mine and tearing a hole in the bomb bay. Landed back at Scampton 0050hrs.

F/S Cyril Anderson
AJ-Y, ED924/G experienced navigational difficulties and malfunction of rear turret. Turned back over Germany at 0310hrs without dropping mine. Landed back at Scampton 0530hrs with mine still onboard.

The Lancaster of P/O Vernon Byers (AJ-K) was hit by flak on the way to the dams and crashed into the Waddenzee off the Dutch coast. His name is commemorated on the Commonwealth Air Forces Memorial at Runnymede in Surrey, together with 20,000 other Commonwealth airmen who have no known grave. Of the crew of AJ-K, the body of F/S J. McDowell was the only one to be recovered from the sea.

(Author's collection)

WHAT HAPPENED TO THE AIRCRAFT THAT SURVIVED THE DAMS RAID?

ED825 (AJ-T) – Missing, arms supply drop to SOE target in northern France, 10-12-43. Hit by flak when flying at low level and crashed.

ED886 (AJ-O) – Missing, arms supply drop to SOE target in northern France, 10-12-43. Hit by flak and crashed at Terramesnil, Somme.

ED906 (AJ-J) – To 61 Sqn, 08-46. SOC 29-07-47

ED909 (AJ-P) – To 61 Sqn. Instructional airframe 6242M. SOC 29-07-47.

ED912 (AJ-N) – To 46 MU, 02-45. SOC 29-06-46.

ED918 (AJ-F) – Struck sea and crashed into sea wall, Snettisham, Norfolk, on practice low-level night bombing exercise, 20-01-44.

ED921 (AJ-W) – Damaged 17-08-44. Stored 46 MU. SOC 26-09-47

ED924 (AJ-Y) – Damaged 02-07-44. Stored 46 MU. SOC 23-09-46.

ED929 (AJ-L) – Stored 46 MU, 01-45. SOC 07-10-46.

ED932 (AJ-G) – To 61 Sqn. SOC 29-07-47.

ED936 (AJ- H) – Damaged 21-07-44. SOC 28-07-44.

KEY

MU = Maintenance Unit

SOC = Struck off Charge (scrapped)

SOE = Special Operations Executive

WHAT HAPPENED TO THE DAMS RAID SURVIVORS?

O f the 133 men who set out on the dams raid, seventy-seven returned. And of these survivors, thirty-two were destined not to see out the war's end. They include W/C Guy Gibson and his entire crew. Most of these men were still serving with 617 Squadron at the time of their deaths, but in the cases of Gibson, F/S Anderson, F/L Trevor-Roper and F/O Jagger they had moved on to other squadrons in Bomber Command. Their names are listed below.

617 Sqn, KIA, Ladbergen (Dortmund-Ems Canal), 14/15 September 1943
S/L D.J.H. Maltby, Sgt W. Hatton, F/S V. Nicholson, F/O J. Fort, F/S A.J. Stone, F/S V. Hill, Sgt H.T. Simmonds.

617 Sqn, KIA, Ladbergen (Dortmund-Ems Canal), 15/16 September 1943
F/L T.H. Taerum, F/O F.M.Spafford, F/L R.E.G. Hutchison, P/O G.A. Deering, F/L L.G. Knight, Sgt D. Allatson, Sgt D.J.D. Powell.

49 Sqn, KIA, Mannheim, 23/24 September 1943
F/S C.T. Anderson, Sgts D. Paterson, L. Nugent, D. Bickle, G.J. Green, A. Ewan and R. Buck.

617 Sqn, KIA, Liège, 20/21 December 1943
F/S E.C. Smith, F/O R. MacFarlane, WO2 J.W. Thrasher, WO2 C.B. Gowrie, F/S T.W. Maynard, F/S S. Burns.

617 Sqn, KIA, Antheor Viaduct, 12/13 February 1944
F/L R.C. Hay.

617 Sqn, killed in flying accident, 13 February 1944
Sgt J. Pulford.

97 Sqn, KIA Nuremberg, 30/31 March 1944
F/L R.A.D. Trevor-Roper.

460 Sqn, killed in training accident, 30 April 1944
F/O B. Jagger.

627 Sqn, KIA, Rheydt, 19/20 September 1944
W/C G.P. Gibson.

KIA = Killed in Action

INDEX

238